Discovering Acts

Discovering Acts

Josh Wilson

FOREWORD BY
John Lee

RESOURCE *Publications* · Eugene, Oregon

DISCOVERING ACTS

Resource Publications
An Imprint of Wipf and Stock Publishers
199 W. 8th Ave., Suite 3
Eugene, OR 97401

www.wipfandstock.com

PAPERBACK ISBN: 978-1-6667-5972-3
HARDCOVER ISBN: 978-1-6667-5973-0
EBOOK ISBN: 978-1-6667-5974-7

11/17/22

Foreword

Two underrated qualities in our modern age are experience and character. This situation is not surprising. Experience and character cannot be captured in soundbites, short videos; and memes, such is the limitation of a digital age. Furthermore, our media shapes our view of the world and constrains messages, for good and ill. Marshall McLuhan made this point a generation ago—the medium is the message. Historically, this was not always the case.

Experience and character were important, indeed, essential. Consider Plato who argued that leaders must be educated, trained, and tested. Only when people reached fifty were they ready to lead. They were philosopher kings. Also consider the pastoral epistles in the New Testament.

When it comes to qualifications of ecclesiastical offices, the importance of character receives the dominant accent, almost exclusively. There is much wisdom in Plato and the New Testament.

Some kinds of knowledge can only be gained through practice. By and large our tradition emphasizes conceptual understanding at the expense of experiential knowledge and wisdom. If there is a logic of which the logician does not know, then the importance of practice rises. If we take another step and bring in the importance of faith, then experience and character rise still higher. The Bible is the type of book that requires faith and obedience. Only those who have walked down that path understand and can communicate that vision.

I am very pleased to see that Wipf and Stock will publish Josh's work on the book of Acts. I have known Josh Wilson for six years as a colleague. During this time, we have spent countless hours talking about texts, passages, and life. What stands out is Josh's character. He is a devoted father, husband, educator, and friend. He is also humble, loving, and understanding. He does not position himself for praise or seek to be at the center. I suspect that Josh's hours of pouring over the Bible makes all the difference. Josh is also an experienced minister and educator. Not only does he have the degrees to prove it, but more importantly he loves God's people and serves them from the pulpit, in homes over coffee, and certainly in classrooms with young minds, ready to explore the big questions of life. I would want a man like Josh to write a guide for students.

This year, Josh celebrates his forty-fifth birthday, a perfect time to share his insights, life, and love.

John Lee

The Geneva School of Manhattan
New York City, Fall 2022

Preface

This devotional is intended for anyone who is looking for a way to spend time each day in Scripture, from students to adults. It was originally written in weekly installments for the students in my youth group, but after a few weeks I discovered that we were running out of copies. When I investigated I discovered that many of the adults in the church had begun using this Bible study as well. Soon both students and adults were asking about the devotional, and if I happened to be late in delivering it they would ask when it was coming. If it hadn't been for my fellow congregants' expectation every Wednesday that I would provide the next week of studies, I probably would have never finished this book.

At the time it was difficult to find an interactive devotional that immersed the reader in the biblical text and required them to read carefully and search for answers themselves. I think this is still the case. There are a lot of topical books on things like purity or identity or leadership, as well as devotionals that feature an author's thoughts about a few verses and perhaps a nice story or illustration, but very few that are designed as daily readings that take the reader through a book of the Bible from beginning to end. This devotional is designed to do just that, with the goal of fostering Bible study habits that will stick around for years to come.

This project has been a labor of love—love for the Lord and for the church. But the real value of this devotional lies in your own labor. Although I provide a short commentary for each passage, your diligence in searching the text, thinking deeply about the readings, and jotting down what you learn will be transformative. Although I trace a different theme in the questions and commentary for each reading, something entirely different may jump out as you read, something God has for you. When that happens, be sure to go with it. Write down what you are learning, questions you have, and insights you gain. Finally, feel free to annotate your own Bible as you read. It will become a record of your journey through Acts and a resource for years to come.

Introduction

This daily devotional is designed to help you learn to study the Bible on your own. Many devotional guides give inspirational thoughts or stories. Others explain or summarize passages of Scripture. While these can be encouraging and enlightening, it is even more rewarding to learn to read and understand the Bible on your own. Hopefully by using this devotional, you'll learn the important elements of reading the Bible on your own.

This can be an intimidating task. Let's break it up into three steps. We'll use these steps each time we look at a passage.

Observe

It may sound obvious, but the first thing you do when you approach a Bible passage is ask, *"What does it say?"* In this step, don't go beyond the obvious. Read for the facts, and these become our foundation for the next steps. The questions in the observation section will be things you can find in the passage—important things people say, key details about events the author wants to highlight, and other information that you can find just by reading the passage carefully. The Scripture won't have an impact on your life unless you first know what the passage is actually saying.

Interpret

Now take those facts and ask yourself the question, *"What does it mean?"* Your goal here is to make sense of the facts, especially considering what the passage would mean to the original audience. For example, when Paul talks about the "Law" in Romans, he is not talking about the American Constitution. Obviously, since the Constitution was written almost 2,000 after Paul died, his early readers had never heard of the Constitution. Consider what "Law" would have meant to those reading Romans—in this case, the Old Testament law (Genesis-Deuteronomy). The point is, *a passage can't mean to us what it never meant when it was written.*

Also keep in mind the all-important principle of *context.* When you read a passage, don't forget everything else you've read in the Bible. A passage that seems to be saying that you can get saved by doing good works alone should be considered in the context of the whole Bible. Since we know clearly from other passages that salvation can't be accomplished through good works, the passage in question must mean something else.

Also keep in mind the *context* of the passage you are reading. If we're focusing on 5 verses, don't forget what the entire chapter is about, and the rest of the book as well. For example, Leviticus 11 lays out dietary laws for the Israelites at the inception of the Israelite nation-the things they were allowed and not allowed to eat. Just like we don't do everything the Old Testament believers did, we don't necessarily do everything the New Testament believers did either. For example, the context of Acts 2 is the first few months of Christianity. God was employing new methods to spread the gospel—methods that were necessary to quickly ground His church in the First Century. Without considering the *context* of what you're reading, you could apply Scripture in ways God never meant— from not helping your dad mow the lawn on a Saturday to trying out a little (rusty) Spanish in the morning worship service.

Apply

All these steps are useless if you don't *apply* what you've learned to your life. If your interpretation of Acts 5:40–42 is that persecution shouldn't keep you from obeying God, an application might be something general like, "Christians should continue to witness even if the government outlaws it," or more specific, like, "This week I'm going to witness to Frank, even if he thinks I sound like an idiot." Usually, more specific applications are better. That way you can see what you're learning in the Bible impact *your* life in clear, tangible ways. Remember, the only way the Bible is going to make any difference in your life is if you choose to apply it! With that in mind, each devotional includes some space for you to write after the application section. Some days provide more space than others. Maybe you noticed something that isn't mentioned in this devotional, or want to answer some of the questions posed in the application section. Use it as a journal to track your thoughts and how you want to change based on what you have learned.

A few technical notes ...

The translation used for this devotional is the NIV (New International Version), simply because it's so widely used, and it's a good version. Feel free to use any translation you have. The KJV, New KJV, ESV, NASB and some others are good translations as well—you don't need to use an NIV to do this bible study.

Finally, do your best to answer each question on your own. You can do this just by using the passage we're looking at. In the "Interpretation" section, there are often a number of possible answers, based on your observations. Think deeply about these questions and you may be surprised at the new ideas that pop out to you, and how God can simply use what He's written to teach you new things. Before long, you'll be coming to your *own* conclusions about what passages mean, and that's exciting.

Introduction to Acts

No other book is quite like the New Testament book of Acts. We have four different perspectives on Jesus' life in the Gospels, and multiple letters from Paul, as well as letters by other Apostles. But if we want to learn about how the Christian church began and spread, and what the consequences were of telling the world about Jesus, we have to look at Acts. Here are a few details:

- *Written by Luke, the author of the third Gospel*
- *Acts is a continuation of the book of Luke*
- *Luke was a doctor*
- *Holy Spirit mentioned more than 50 times*
- *Acts begins with Jesus' ascension into heaven and ends with Paul as a prisoner in Rome (covers 30+ years)*
- *Acts is the only account of the early church*
- *Good accompanying book to Paul's letters*

If you've ever wondered how to tell someone about your faith in Christ, you'll find the answer in Acts. If you've ever been ridiculed or looked down on for your beliefs, you'll find a new perspective (and encouragement) in Acts. If you've ever wondered how Christianity started, or been skeptical about whether Christianity is even true, you'll find these topics in Acts. Hop on board as we begin to study the foundations of the early church and follow the lives of the people who dared to believe what seemed impossible: that the eternal God became a human, died, and came back to life again, all for the purpose of allowing us to have a relationship with Him, and to be with Him someday in heaven.

Outline of Acts

Acts is one of the few books of the Bible that gives us an outline of the book within the actual text. Read Acts 1:8:

> " . . . but you will receive power when the Holy Spirit comes on you; and you will be my witnesses in *Jerusalem*, and in *Judea and Samaria*, and to the *ends of the earth*."

There are 28 chapters in Acts, which is the story of how the Gospel spread throughout the Mediterranean world. Acts 1:8 shows us the order in which different geographical places were reached with the Gospel. Using 1:8 as an outline, the book breaks down like this:

   I. Witness in **Jerusalem** (1:1–8:4)

  II. Witness in **Judea** and **Samaria** (8:5–12:25)

 III. Witness to the **Remotest Part of the Earth** (chs 13–28)

Also, Acts follows the activity (or "acts") of all the apostles, but mainly two apostles: Peter and Paul. Here are the chapters that deal with each of them:

   I. Peter (chs 1–12)

  II. Paul (chs 13–28)

Notice that this means Peter is mainly a witness to the Jews (Jerusalem, Judea, Samaria) and Paul to the Non-Jews (remotest parts of the earth). Keep these outlines in mind. They provide an easy way to remember how the Gospel first spread.

Read 1:1–8

Observe

Who is Acts written to?

How long was Jesus on earth after his crucifixion?

*We are told a few different things Jesus did during that time.
List as many of these things as you can:*

What does Jesus command the disciples to do (v.4)?

Interpret

Why would Jesus stay on earth for 40 days after His crucifixion?

What details about Jesus might have convinced the Apostles that He did indeed rise from the dead?

Read verse 8. Why do you think it was a priority for Jesus to convince His disciples that He was alive—risen from the dead?

Apply

Did you know that of the 12 apostles in the book of Acts, 11 of them went on to be martyred for their belief in Christ? Only John lived to a ripe old age. What does this have to do with Acts 1? If you didn't notice, Jesus made sure the Apostles had ample evidence that He was alive, after they had all seen him crucified. This was because of what Jesus commands in verse 8. Read this verse again.

What about you? *Are you convinced you know who Jesus Christ was (and is)?* Jesus's command to the Apostles to be witnesses is a command to you as well. If you're not convinced Jesus literally rose from the dead, you're not equipped to reach others with the Gospel. On a scale from 1–10 (10 being the highest), how convinced are you of Jesus's literal resurrection? Based on these verses, how do you believe God would have you respond to the fact of His resurrection?

Read 1:9–14

Observe

What is the last thing the Apostles see Jesus do on earth?

What question do the two angels ask the Apostles?

What are the Apostles told will someday happen (v.11)?

In verse 13, how many Apostles are present?

Interpret

Stop and picture in your mind what happens in verse 9. If you were Theophilus (the man Acts is written to), how would you respond to what Luke writes in verse 9?

Why do you think the angels ask the Apostles the question in verse 11? Read this verse again. What point do you think they are trying to make?

Apply

We're told in verse 14 that immediately after Christ's ascension into heaven, the Apostles and women with them "joined together constantly in prayer." I doubt it was with a feeling of reluctance or drudgery they did this. They had just seen Jesus rise into heaven before their very eyes!

When the angels ask the Apostles in verse 11 why they are just looking at the sky, their point is this: *Jesus is coming back someday in the same way he left. Get busy!* Notice that they immediately go back to Jerusalem to pray and attend to other business. *Have you forgotten that Jesus will return someday to earth? How can this truth impact your life this week?*

Read 1:15–20

Observe

Who seems to emerge here as the leader of the apostles?

Verse 16 contains a phrase that serves as a great description of what we call "inspiration" of the Bible. Try to identify that phrase and write it below.

What does Peter do to show that what happened to Judas, and to their group of disciples, was part of God's will?

Interpret

Consider the phrase you noted in verse 16 as being a statement of how all Scripture (not just Psalms) came about. When you read the Bible, whose thoughts are you reading?

Why does Peter choose at this point to look back and quote from the Old Testament?

Apply

Here in Acts 1, we're looking in at the first Christian group to ever exist. It's a small group; we're told about 120 strong (v. 15). This group has embraced the truth—that the man they knew on earth, Jesus Christ, had die, and had physically come back to life again. It hit them that this man was literally God! And they chose to believe something very unpopular; that this man, who was God, had come to offer forgiveness of sin and eternity with God.

The apostles and early Christians were facing a daunting future; to hold to what they believed, even though it was so unpopular and unbelievable to those around them. What they faced is not unlike what you probably face each day. Have you forgotten the significance of your beliefs? The apostles stood out from those around them. Do you? *What can you do this week to stand out as a Christian in your school, work or group of friends. Let the example of these early Christians challenge you.*

Read 1:21–26

Observe

What is the task Peter tells them they need to undertake?

On what does he base his decision to do this (vv. 16 and 20)?

What is the qualification for this new disciple?

Interpret

The sole qualification for the new apostle is found in verses 21–22. There were only 12 apostles. Why do you think this was a qualification for being an apostle?

How do the apostles make their decision of how to elect as the next apostle (there are two things in vv. 24–25)?

Apply

As we read the book of Acts, it's important to remember that when the action takes place, the Gospels (Matthew, Mark, Luke, John) have not been written yet. Why does this matter? Well, the main qualification for being the twelfth apostle was that he had witnessed Jesus's earthly ministry and had seen Jesus after his resurrection. Sharing this news is how the gospel first spread. Not by people reading about Jesus in the gospels, but by word of mouth. The apostles could say, "I knew this man, I was with him for three years. He never sinned, he performed miracles, he died, and rose again!"

The best way to reach your friends and acquaintances for Jesus is to do this same thing. In Acts, it was about Jesus Christ—defending and spreading the truth about Him. It's *still* about Jesus. The apostles could say they intimately knew Jesus. Can you say that? *What can you do today to have a better relationship with Christ?*

Read 2:1–13

Observe

The Holy Spirit empowers the believers to do something amazing here. What is that?

Are the languages the believers speak actual languages that were foreign to them, or were they just meaningless ramblings? How do you know? (v.8)

Interpret

What seems to be the purpose of this miracle?

Considering Jesus had ascended only a few months ago, why is this a good time for this miracle?

Read Luke 24:49. What do you think this verse has to do with the passage we just read from Acts?

Apply

This is an extremely important portion of the New Testament. In the Old Testament, we're told very little about the third person of the Trinity, the Holy Spirit. Here, the Spirit makes an amazing entrance into the lives of Christians. If you've read carefully, you probably noted that the Spirit enabled the Christians to speak fluently in languages they didn't know. This would be like you suddenly speaking Russian or Arabic. Can you imagine that? This was a true miracle.

So what was its purpose? One hint is in verses 9–11. In Jerusalem there were people who spoke many foreign languages. How are all these people going to hear the Gospel if nobody knows their language? God chose to empower the Christians to speak foreign languages, in order to quickly spread the Gospel of His Son. Jesus promised this would happen back in Luke 24:49. (Take a moment and look up this verse.) As we work through Acts we'll see the results of this. Let this passage begin to form the basis of what you know about the Holy Spirit. Like all issues, what we believe about the Spirit should be Biblical.

Read 2:14–21

Observe

Who is Peter speaking to here?

Peter tells everyone that the "men are not . . . " what?

Who does Peter quote in verses 17–21?

Interpret

As noted in the introduction to this study, Peter was a missionary to the Jews. What advantage might a Jew have over a non-Jew when hearing the Gospel Peter is going to preach here?

Why does Peter say the men are not drunk? Why would anyone think that?

What parts of Joel's prophecy (especially in vv. 17–18) look like what happened at the beginning of this chapter? Is there anything in that prophecy that seems like it doesn't fit what has happened so far?

Apply

You've just begun to read Peter's sermon, which goes to verse 39. This sermon is regarded as the first major event in church history, and it led to 3,000 conversions! Notice that Peter is speaking to Jews. A Jew would have the advantage of knowing much of the Old Testament, which predicted Christ's coming, death, and resurrection. Therefore, they should have more readily accepted what Peter was saying about Jesus. (We'll see later that this isn't always the case, and God makes the Gospel available to all, not just the Jews.) In Joel's prophecy, God's Spirit is poured out on people, which points to what happens at the beginning of Acts 2. His prophecy goes on to talk about things that are still future even for us (see vv. 19–21). Peter is able to use Scripture to explain what is happening. He quotes it from memory. *Are you familiar enough with Scripture to use it as Peter did? What practical steps can you take to grow in this area?*

Read 2:22–24

Observe

Peter continues here with his famous sermon. According to verse 22, what made it clear that Jesus had come from God?

What does Peter accuse the Jews of doing?

True or False: It was God's plan for Jesus to be handed over to the Jews and crucified.

Interpret

Peter makes the amazing statement in verse 24 that God raised Jesus from the dead. This is a much-debated fact. Read the following verses and jot down how each verse may strengthen your belief that Jesus rose again:

Jn. 20:6–8

Jn. 20:25-28

1 Cor. 15:6

Apply

Hopefully at this point you've recognized how bold Peter was to say what he said to the Jews. First he accused them of being responsible for Jesus' death, and then he suggested the unthinkable: Jesus had risen from the dead! What makes a person so bold? Peter, as well as many others, had seen Jesus alive after he had been crucified, and this drowned out all his fear. Once he saw the power of God there was no fear of man left in him.

As John 20:68 shows, the tomb was empty. Was Jesus's body stolen, as some suggest? No. The Roman soldiers were bribed to say this. Besides, would the robbers have really taken the time to meticulously fold Jesus's clothes (20:6, 7)? In John 20:25-28, even the skeptic Thomas believed when he saw Jesus, and 1 Corinthians 15:6 tells us that 500 saw the resurrected Jesus—after He'd been crucified—*at the same time!* What about you? *Have you grasped that Jesus rose again, and allowed it to change your life?* Before you end today, read Jesus's words to doubting Thomas in John 20:29. "Those" here refers to you.

Read 2:25–36

Observe

Who does Peter quote here, and from what book of the Bible?

Who is the person Peter quotes speaking about?

According to verse 30, what had God promised to King David?

Interpret

Considering verse 27, why do you think Peter points out in verse 29 that David died and that his tomb is there?

In verses 32–33, Peter tells us 3 things that are true about Jesus. Can you identify these 3 things?

1)

2)

3)

Apply

You've just finished reading Peter's sermon. Next time we'll learn about the effect his sermon had on the Jews who listened. Before we leave it though, you should see how Peter goes about convincing the people of the truth of the Gospel. Verse 36, the last thing Peter says, sums up his message to them. *Read this verse again.*

Peter quotes David, whom all the Jews would have greatly respected. He shows in verses 25–28 that David predicted that the "Holy One" (Jesus) would rise again. Peter tells them that obviously, David's body decayed like any other person (v. 29), and so what David says must refer to someone else. In verses 32–33, Peter leaves us with the facts that God raised Jesus from the dead, Jesus is now at the right hand of God, and that the speaking in tongues they had all just witnessed was in fact the work of Jesus Himself! Notice Peter's boldness in verse 36. He was 100% convinced of what he believed. Are you that convinced? If not, *how do you think you can become more convinced, like Peter was?* If you are, are you sharing the truth with others as Peter did? *Jot down the name (or initials) of one person you know who needs Christ.*

Read 2:37–41

Observe

What effect does Peter's sermon have on those who hear it?

What does Peter tell them to do in response to his sermon (v. 38)?

Interpret

Peter tells the people to (1) repent and (2) be baptized, in order to be forgiven of their sins. Do you think it necessary to be baptized to know you are going to heaven? Support your answer with reasons.

In verse 40, Peter calls his society a "corrupt generation." Based on what he's said in his sermon in chapter 2, why would he call it this? Are there any ways our own society resembles this "corrupt generation?"

Apply

Peter's message was very effective; it says that 3,000 were saved as a result. That's a lot of people—well over 10 times more people than an average-sized American church has on a Sunday morning, and all of them getting saved.

So is baptism necessary for salvation? The answer is no. Remember to consider the whole Bible and avoid coming to conclusions based one a single verse. We know from other verses (see Eph 2:8–9) that the only thing necessary for salvation is faith in Christ. Also, remember that the thief hanging next to Jesus put his faith in Christ while he was on the cross and died before he had a chance to be baptized. However, we should take Peter's two commands here seriously. *First*, he says to repent. That means to "turn around." If you've really put your faith in Jesus, you've turned around from the ways you would live without Him. *Have you done that? If not, your "faith" in Christ might not be faith at all, but just meaningless talk. Second*, if you are confident in your salvation, *have you been baptized?* It doesn't save you, but it's very important—even Jesus did it (Luke 3:21). If you haven't yet been baptized, talk with someone in your church or in your home about taking this step. It's how you show everyone what you really believe.

Read 2:42–47

Observe

Below, list as many characteristics of the early church as you can, based on these six verses.

Interpret

In your opinion, do these things characterize your church? Be specific; below, list those things that DO characterize your church. Are there any ways the early church seems different from yours? If so, list some of those things as well.

Apply

At the beginning of this study, you learned that Acts is the story of how the early church began and spread. We found that Acts would tell us what the early church was like. These six verses go a long way in accomplishing that. Consider these things that were a part of the early church: *learning from the apostles, fellowship, communion, prayer, miracles, extreme generosity, meetings every day, praise for God, growth.*

Most of these things should *still* be part of our church. Instead of learning from the apostles, we need to be learning from the Bible. Communion and "breaking of bread" both refer to the bread and the cup Christians partake in. We're told there were "wonders and miraculous signs." We know from other passages that the ability to perform miracles was unique gift given by God to the 12 apostles. *Of the eight remaining characteristics, choose the two that you do a good job with. Then write two below that you could improve.* Do you spend enough time in prayer? Are you generous with what God has given you? Are you engaged in worship on Sundays in your heart and mind, worshiping, praying, learning? Now get *specific*: How can you improve in these areas this week? They were vital for the early church, and they're important for you too.

Read 3:1–10

Observe

How long had the crippled man been in his condition?

What does Peter say to the man that causes him to be able to stand and walk?

Interpret

How do you think Peter was able to perform this amazing miracle?

Why do you think God empowered the apostles to do miracles like this (you could give a number of possible answers; list as many as you can)?

Apply

Back in *1:8* we read that Jesus told the apostles they would receive power from the Holy Spirit. Yesterday we read in *2:43* that many miracles were performed. Here, we see our first miracle in Acts. Notice that in *1:8*, Jesus is talking to the apostles, and that *2:43* says that "many wonders and miraculous signs were done by the *apostles.*" It was only the apostles who were empowered to perform miracles at this point in Acts.

There are different opinions among Christians about whether or not current-day believers can perform acts of healing, and there are good, godly people on both sides of the question. Whatever you believe is the answer to the question, "Can Christians today perform acts of healing," it is important to approach the question through Scripture. One of the things that made healings so powerful is that the people who observed them could not deny that a miracle had taken place. In today's passage, a man is healed who had been crippled since birth. He had never walked in his entire life. Also notice that the apostles insist that it was God's power, not their own, that worked the miracles. So a final lesson today is about humility. Whether God performs a miracle through a human agent or uses you to encourage someone having a terrible day, it's about God's power.

Read 3:11–26

Observe

What effect does the miracle performed in 3:1–10 have on the people?

What four things (maybe five) does Peter accuse the people of in verses 13b–15?

Interpret

Why do you think Peter mentions Pilate (the Roman governor at Jesus' trial), and the fact that he wanted to let Jesus go free?

This set of verses begins with a question, which is not answered until the end of the section (verse 16). What seems to be the question on the people's minds in verse 12? And what is Peter's answer to this question in verse 16?

Apply

It's been rightly said that the only thing necessary to disprove the resurrection is to produce the body of Christ. In over 2,000 years, those who so desperately want to disprove Christianity have never produced the body of Jesus. Of course, this is because it was resurrected and He is now physically in heaven. In this second sermon of Peter's, he appeals to this in verse 15 when he says, "We are witnesses of this." You also are a witness of this, since you know what the Gospels say about the death and resurrection of Jesus. *Does your response resemble the hard-heartedness of the Jews that called for Jesus death, or the responsiveness of thousands who believed in Christ as a result of this sermon?*

Peter was bold! He told the people that they had handed over Jesus to be killed, released a murderer, and killed the author of life. To make it worse, the unbelieving Pilate was the only one who called for Jesus' release. *In what ways can you be more bold this week in standing for what's right?*

Read 3:17–26

Observe

What was the purpose of the people acting in ignorance?

What did Peter ask the people to do as a result of what he's telling them?

In verse 25, what promise does Peter say God made to Abraham?

Interpret

What the people had done in crucifying Christ involved confusion about who he was. After reading this passage, describe this confusion the best you can. And, what was the right perspective about who He was (and is)?

Interpret verse 25. What did God mean when he promised Abraham "Through your offspring all peoples of the earth will be blessed"?

Apply

Peter ends by mentioning the promise God made to Abraham (though Peter is arrested before his sermon is over). Abraham was the father of the Jewish faith and nationality, and through him came Jesus. Through Jesus came eternal life to everyone who would believe in Him. So through Abraham, people from all nations of the earth are blessed.

Throughout this last portion of his sermon (before he is interrupted and put in jail), Peter talks a lot about what the Old Testament prophets had said. His point is that, although the people had sinned and acted in ignorance, what they had done fulfilled many Old Testament prophecies about Jesus' death. In other words, even though they had sinned in crucifying Christ, it was exactly what God had planned and foretold through the prophets. Its purpose, of course, was to provide a means for forgiveness of sin. God may also use mistakes you make in your own life to work out his plan for you. *What mistakes have you made in your past? What might God be trying to teach you through those things?*

Read 4:1–12

Observe

Why were Peter and John thrown into jail?

According to verse 8, how was Peter able to face the Sanhedrin so boldly?

Interpret

Why do you think it was "disturbing" to the priests and Sadducees that the apostles were claiming Jesus had risen from the dead?

In verse 11, Peter quotes Psalm 118:22. Turn back in your Bible and read this verse in its original context. How does this verse relate to what you know about Christ?

Apply

By this time you have probably noticed how much Peter quoted from Scripture. We saw yesterday that he talked a lot about the prophets and pointed out that what happened to Christ was predicted in the prophets. In today's study, he does this again; the verse from Psalm 118 is one the Jewish priests surely knew; they would have had much of the Old Testament memorized. Yet they failed to understand what it meant. Peter is showing them how much of the Old Testament applies to this man, Jesus Christ. He is dealing with the priests and teachers on their own turf.

The Sanhedrin was basically the Jewish Supreme Court, made up of 71 of the most respected, well learned Jewish priests and teachers of the law. Why was Peter's preaching that Christ was crucified so disturbing to the Sanhedrin? As John MacArthur explains, "They had executed Christ as a blasphemer and now Peter and John were proclaiming His resurrection." Imagine Peter standing before the people and saying, "Do you remember the man the Sanhedrin executed? He was God's son, the one the Scriptures promised would come!" Do you get it? The Sanhedrin knew that if Peter was right, they were on the wrong side of history. What about you? Are you on the right side? It's about more than just going to church; it means being true to Christ in what you say and do, even when it's tough. *Determine this week; even tomorrow, to be a Peter or a John.*

Read 4:13–22

Observe

What was it that surprised the Sanhedrin about Peter and John?

Describe the tough situation the Sanhedrin found themselves in, as described in verses 16–22:

In verses 18–20, do Peter and John say they will obey their government, or obey God?

Interpret

Turn ahead to 1 Corinthians 1:18–20. How does this passage apply to what you read today in Acts? Specifically, focus on the issue of wisdom (that of Peter and John).

Peter and John say point blank they will obey God instead of the Sanhedrin. What is the Sanhedrin asking of them that Peter and John are refusing to do?

Apply

Can you imagine all this fuss over one man being healed? Since the beginning of Chapter 3 Acts has been talking about this one man who was healed and the backlash it caused. We just saw in verse 16 that "everybody living in Jerusalem" had heard about what the apostles had done, and that everyone was praising God, because the man was 40 years old (v. 22). This was truly a miracle! It put the Sanhedrin in an awkward situation. They couldn't deny how wonderful the miracle was, but the apostles preached a message alongside that miracle that was very annoying to the Sanhedrin: unbelieving Jews had executed the Lord.

Read again verses 18–20. Peter and John say right in front of the Sanhedrin that they refuse to stop preaching the name of Jesus. *What do you think Peter and John will do? When do you think it is right to disobey those in authority?*

Read 4:23–31

Observe

Peter and John reported back to the other Christians and reported what the priests and elders had said to them. Look back at yesterday's passage (4:13–22). Exactly what did they say to them?

Verses 25b–26 quote David's words in Psalms. There is a word used in verse 27 that is also used in this quotation by David? What is that word, and who does it apply to?

According to verse 28, were those who put Jesus to death (Herod and Pontius Pilate) carrying out their own will, or God's?

Interpret

Do Peter and John's attitude seem to be one of fear, after being threatened by the priests and elders? If not, how would you describe their attitude?

What did the Christians ask God for in verses 29-30? What seems to be their priority?

Apply

What a powerful scene. Peter and John have just been brought before the most powerful court in Jerusalem, and what is their response? They go tell the other Christians, and then praise God and ask for greater boldness in preaching Christ. You can almost sense the atmosphere: Christianity is brand new, and this relatively small band of believers are outsiders, rebels, saying what no one wants to believe or hear. But they don't back down from their message. *Do you sense this attitude in your own life?*

Notice that they pray for greater boldness. In part, this is because they've recognized that God predicted what was going to happen to Christ, and what the response would be. *Do you pray for boldness in witnessing to your friends? Before you end today, take a moment and pray that you would be more confident, and bold enough to share Christ with those around you.*

Read 4:32–37

Observe

Describe what life was like as part of the early church, from this passage:

Besides "Joseph," what other name was given to Joseph?

What does that name mean, according to the passage?

Interpret

What do you think caused the believers to be so generous with their possessions?

What was the message they were preaching, according to vs. 33? How do you think the Christians' lifestyle affected how people perceived their message? In other words, what effect do you think their lifestyle had on their sharing of the Gospel?

Apply

If I were to give this day's devotional a title, it would be "Priorities," because at this point in the Christian church, the believers had their priorities right! Notice what they've committed themselves to: First, they *share everything they have.* If anyone is in need, they make sure they meet that person's need. We're told some even sold land and gave the money to the apostles to be distributed *Do we do a good job of meeting the needs of those in our church? Do you personally take notice of the needs of others?*

Second, what is the other priority? Verse 33 tells us that they continued to *preach the resurrection of Christ.* "Much grace" was upon them all, meaning they had favor from people outside the church, due to their love and unity. What a powerful combination! Generosity towards each other, coupled with preaching Christ resurrected. They weren't just telling the world about Jesus' love, they were showing it.

Read 5:1–11

Observe

Describe the sin Ananias and Sapphira committed.

What effect did God's judgment have on the other Christians?

Interpret

Besides Satan (v. 3), what may have motivated this husband and wife to lie about how much they were giving to the apostles (see vv. 36–37)?

God's punishment may seem overly severe. Why do you think God chose to judge this sin the way He did?

Apply

Up to this point, the books of Acts has been fairly positive. We've seen thousands get saved. The Holy Spirit has empowered the apostles to advance the gospel, including working miracles. Persecution has not discouraged the Christians, but strengthened their faith and resolve. But here in chapter 5, we have the first mention of two who aren't on board; in essence, they're imposters!

Note that the sin of Ananias and Sapphira isn't that they kept some money back—it was after all their money, which they received for selling land. The problem was that they lied and said they were giving everything to the church. God probably wouldn't choose to judge a sin like this with death, in our own day. But the church was growing, and the Christians were being a great example to the world. God didn't want the selfishness of these two to creep into the church—though clearly that was Satan's goal (v. 3).

If there's one thing we can take from this story, it's that we should take our own honesty—especially in our giving to the church—very seriously! *Are you honest about how you use your money? What steps can you take this week to be sure you're giving with an honest heart?*

Read 5:12–24

Observe

Who was performing signs and wonders?

What causes the high priest and Sadducees to arrest the apostles? E.g., what motivates them to do this (v. 17–18)?

For what purpose does the angel free the apostles from prison (vs. 19–21)

Interpret

Read verses 12–13 again. Why do you think it says "no one else dared join them?"

How do the apostles respond to the angel's command in verse 20? Be as specific as possible.

Apply

Have you ever been in or seen a church built in the middle ages? One of those beautiful, huge architectural wonders, with beautiful stained glass and intricate carvings? Those types of cathedrals are all over Europe. It shows how established Christianity was in Europe. The same can be said here in the States, though our churches are not usually as ornate. You and I have grown up taking Christianity for granted; it's always been around, and we can see the evidence of its history. Here in Acts, we're going back to the foundations of Christianity! The Christians have nowhere to meet except Solomon's Colonnade (an outdoor court with pillars). The gospel is being opened to everyone who will accept it, and the apostles are working tirelessly to preach, teach, and do miracles.

Why does no one dare to join the Christians meeting together (v. 13)? Well, consider the persecution they've gone through for believing in Jesus. We're told that even though the apostles are "highly regarded," many feared the consequences of becoming a Christian. *Would you have followed Christ in light of possible persecution? Do you continue to follow Him even though it may mean losing friends, or ridicule?*

Read 5:25–42

Observe

The Sanhedrin (group of 71 religious leaders) seem intent on putting the apostles to death? Gamaliel asks them to reconsider. Summarize his argument to the Sanhedrin:

What does the Sanhedrin do to the apostles before letting them go?

What does the Sanhedrin demand of the apostles before letting them go?

Interpret

Why do you think the Sanhedrin wants to kill the apostles (v. 30)? There may be a few possible answers.

Why is verse 42 so surprising?

Apply

Would you be willing to be tortured or even killed for your belief in Jesus? I've often wondered this about myself. You and I may never have the chance to be tortured for Christ, as the apostles were (they counted it an amazing privilege—see v. 42). But, that only means God is asking something different of us. Right now he isn't looking for us to *die* for Him, but to *live* for Him!

The apostles had the right perspective in life—they knew God had given them time on earth so they could give it back to Him. And don't they seem happy? *Have you really given your life to Christ? Or do you just say you believe Him but live your own way?* What makes you think you would die for Him if you're not willing to live for Him? *Below, write one specific thing you can do this week (and make part of your weekly routine) to prove that you really do have faith in Christ, and it's not just words. Witness to that friend, begin tithing regularly, spend a few moments each morning in prayer, change the music you're choosing to listen to, get rid of a bad habit—whatever God is calling you to do!*

Read 6:1–7

Observe

Describe the problem these verses describe, as you understand it.

What do the Apostles do to fix the problem?

What do they think is not the right way to handle the problem?

Interpret

Why do you think the apostles chose to find other people to do the work that was needed, instead of doing it themselves?

What were the qualifications of the people that were chosen? In other words, what did the Apostles say needs to be true of the men they choose?

One man is talked about more than the others. Who is this, and how is he described (see v. 5)?

Apply

In verse 1, you may have the term "Grecian Jews" or "Hellenistic Jews." These terms refer to an Israelite (Jew) who lived in the Greek culture. Some true Israelites may have been opposed to the Greek lifestyle some of these Jews had. Maybe the Greek Jews felt they were being overlooked because of their cultural background. Whatever the case, the Apostles decide that preaching the gospel is too important to set aside; we're told at the beginning of the chapter that the number of Christians is continuing to increase. The apostles seem to make a good decision in this chapter, because notice how the end of our section ends (v. 7). The word of God continues to spread after their decision.

One name sticks out among the others: Stephen, a man "full of faith and of the Holy Spirit" (v. 5). Stephen was the best of the best; he rose to the top even among those who were considered the most Spirit-filled. *How do you know when someone is full of faith? Below, describe what that would look like. Would someone describe you as a man/woman of faith?*

Read 6:8–15

Observe

This section begins by describing someone we learned about yesterday. Who was that person, and how was he described in yesterday's section?

How is he described here?

Interpret

There are three groups that have a problem with Stephen. What seems to be their gripe against him?

They make up a lie about Stephen. What is that lie? Turn to and read Leviticus 24:16. What does this verse have to do with the passage we're reading today?

Apply

The reaction the members of the synagogues have to Stephen is similar to their reaction to Jesus. They can't stand up against Stephen in a normal debate. Ever seen a formal debate at school? Imagine something like that. So what do they do? They find people to lie about things he has said and try to accuse him of blasphemy. This is a very dirty way to attack Stephen—these "religious" men compromised their character and destroyed someone's reputation, all for the purpose of killing him. There are two things we can learn from this passage.

First, it's been said, "Watch your character, and your reputation will take care of itself." The point is, you can't help what people say about you, but you can make sure you're doing what's right. That's what Stephen did. Second, telling lies about people can destroy lives. Are you being careful about what you say about others? What you say will stick with people long after you've forgotten what you even said. Do you find yourself hurting people's character through what you say about them? Which of these two most applies to your life? Pick one and ask God to help you remember and work on that truth this week.

Read 7:1-60

For today and tomorrow, we're going to do something different. Acts 7 is one of the most amazing chapters in the Bible, for many reasons. Instead of telling you what to see in this chapter, I'd rather you read it for yourself. If you can, read this chapter in one sitting. *Pay close attention to the words Stephen speaks, and how the religious leaders reacted to him.*

After you've read through the chapter once, summarize each of these sections in one sentence or phrase. We'll take 3 days to cover the chapter, so read carefully; there's a lot packed into this section, and a lot you can learn! As you summarize each section in one sentence, keep in mind you are tracing the history of the Jewish people.

7:1-4

7:5-8

7:9-10

7:11-16

7:17-19

Read 7:1–60

Read this chapter once again, then go ahead and jot down one sentence for each section that sums up what you read.

7:20–26

7:27–29

7:30–34

7:35–38

7:39–43

7:44–50

Read 7:51–60

Observe

What does Stephen accuse the religious leaders of? There are a few possible answers.

What has caused Stephen to give such a long, passion-filled answer to his accusers? What was he accused of (see chapter 6)?

Interpret

Why do you think Stephen has described so much of Israel's history, as he stands before the religious leaders?

The religious leaders are angry in verse 54. What makes them angry? What ultimately causes them to execute Peter?

Apply

Stephen is the very first Christian martyr in history. As we saw a few days ago in Leviticus 24:16, the punishment for blasphemy is death, according to Old Testament law. But is this a true execution, or a violent mob killing? What is it about Stephen that brings out such seething hatred from these religious leaders?

Stephen shows that he knows the Old Testament fluidly, as he describes the details of Israel's past. The high priest and other leaders can't accuse him of ignorance. He shows he's not just a Greek, but a true Jew. Remember what brought Stephen to this courtroom? 6:13 says that "they produced false witnesses" to testify lies about Stephen, making him sound anti-Jewish.

Instead of defending himself, Stephen dives into a blatant attack on the Jewish leaders, probably knowing he'll be executed as a result. His main point is in 7:52. Read that verse again. His point is that historically, the Jewish religious leaders have always resisted true prophets of God, usually killing them! And of course, the same is true of how they responded to Jesus.

Stephen is telling them they're on the wrong side of history once again. He accuses them of "betraying and murdering" Jesus! I imagine that didn't sit well with the religious leaders. Before leaving this chapter, consider the amazing boldness of Stephen. We were told in chapter 6 that Stephen was a man of faith. *Do you have the passion and faith that Stephen had when it came to what he believed? Would you die for your faith, as Stephen did?*

Read 8:1–8

Observe

Where were the Christians scattered to (excepting the Apostles)?

Find these locations (including Jerusalem) on a map, and draw arrows showing how the Christians were scattered. (Hint: Check the last few pages of your Bible for a map.)

Who is leading the persecution against the church? What kinds of things is he doing?

Interpret

Do you remember what Acts 1:8 said? We saw that it was the outline for the book of Acts. Read this verse again. How does what you read today continue to play out Acts 1:8?

What was the response of the Christians who were scattered? In other words, what did they do?

Apply

When Saul began to drag Christians out of their houses and throw them in jail, the remaining Christians got scared, hid, and stopped telling others about Jesus. Right? Wrong. We see in verse 4 that, while the Christians did scatter to avoid being thrown in prison, they continued to preach the gospel. It's the only thing they could do. Most of these people were new Christians. They had accepted the truth about Jesus, who had just died not long ago, and that had changed their lives. They didn't have anything else to do with their lives; they couldn't deny their beliefs and settle into a comfortable life, living each day for themselves. Christ had changed everything for them, and certainly the threat of being thrown into jail was no match to stop them from telling others about Christ. *Are there things in your life that are more important to you than your witness for Christ? If so, list them below. What can you do to change these proprieties?*

Do you see Acts 1:8 playing out now, like we learned about a few weeks ago? Jesus told the disciples they would be his "witnesses" in Jerusalem, Judea and Samaria, and to the ends of the earth. Over the last few weeks we've seen their witness in Jerusalem. Now we see that God has scattered them to be witnesses in Judea and Samaria, as verse 4 mentions. Soon, we will see how God raises up a man to be a witness to the ends of the earth.

Read 8:9–25

Observe

Describe Simon.

What do we learn about him in verse 13?

What does he ask for in verse 19?

Interpret

In verses 14–17, what do Peter and John come to Samaria to do?

Do you think Simon's belief was genuine? Read John 2:23–24. How might this passage from John apply to what we've read about Simon?

Apply

In verse 15, we're told that Peter and John "came down" to Samaria, but notice the map we looked at yesterday. Samaria is actually north of Jerusalem. Why does it say they came down? Whenever the Bible talks about Jerusalem, you are always "going down" when you leave, and "coming up" when you enter. This is because Jerusalem is set on a hill, and everything is down in elevation compared to it. Keep this in mind as you read Acts, and other books.

Something troubling happens to Simon in this passage. You should realize we're not talking about the Apostle Simon, but a sorcerer in Samaria, who impressed people through his magic. We're told in verse 13 "Simon himself also believed . . . ", but later, in verse 19, he shows that he hasn't really believed.

John 2:23–24 tell us that some believed in Jesus, but that Jesus didn't "commit Himself" to them, because he knew they were just enthusiastic about his miracles. Such is the case with Simon. He tried to buy the power of God with money, and Peter concludes in verse 21 that his heart is "not right in the sight of God." He just want to impress people and make money from them.

They key here is the first word of verse 22. Write that word here:

Keep this word in mind, because it appears as though you can believe Jesus but not truly *repent*, which is what Peter told Simon to do. *Take a look at your life. Do you just believe in Jesus, or have you truly repented (turned around)? If you've repented, it will show in your life: what, and who, you're living for!*

Read 8:26–40

Observe

How did Philip know to go south, and to talk to the Ethiopian eunuch?

What book of the Bible is the Ethiopian reading?

What does he request of Philip?

Interpret

Read 1 Peter 3:15. What phrase in this verse does Philip show he is able to apply in his life?

Apply

This is a good time to talk about an issue that may have come up as you read this passage for today. Do you have verse 37 in your translation? If you're using an NIV, you may have noticed that verse was left out. Why? The verse divisions of every translation follow the King James Version, but the original manuscripts the translators used for the KJV are different than the ones the NIV translators used. The earlier manuscripts, which the NIV uses, do not contain verse 37. You may notice this in other New Testament passages as we continue our study.

Perhaps the most important thing to take from today's passage has to do with 1 Peter 3:15, which tells us to always be ready "to give a reason for the hope that you have." You see, the best way to witness is to answer those who ask you about your faith. If someone is asking questions (as the Ethiopian here did), it means they are open to what you have to say. The Ethiopian wondered about a passage from Isaiah, which had to do with Jesus being compared to a lamb, who was led silently to the slaughter. It's about his crucifixion. Philip found himself in a perfect position to share the gospel! *Are you ready to answer those who ask you about your faith? Or are you more likely to stumble over your words or pretend like you don't know much about Christianity?* Take a moment and think about how you would answer if a friend asked you this: "Why are you a Christian?"

Read 8:13–24 *and* 8:30–40

Observe

These passages represent two "conversions" we read about in chapter 8 of Acts. The first was Simon's conversion. List 3 important points about what we read about Simon:

The second is the Ethiopian's conversion. List 3 important points about what we read about the Ethiopian:

Interpret

It's no accident that these two "conversions" are right near each other in the book of Acts. It's impossible to tell what's really in a person's heart, but which of these do you think might be a true conversion?

Read Matt. 7:21–23. What causes you to think one of these two might be a true conversion to Christianity and the other a false one?

Apply

Does it scare you to read in Matthew 7 that some may think they're going to heaven when they die, when in reality they are going to hell? And that these people even consider themselves believers in Christ? It should! The difference between false and true belief is illustrated in the two "conversions" we looked at today. Simon was impressed with the apostles' miracles, and he wanted part of the action. He may have even believed God gave them their power, and claimed he believed in Jesus. What was missing was true *repentance* (v. 22). To repent means "to turn around."

In contrast, the Ethiopian was not awed by miracles, because he didn't witness any. Instead, he read the Scripture, tried to understand what it meant, and found someone to *teach* him the truth about Jesus. As a result, he trusted Jesus as his savior; not for the popularity he could gain, but because the truth had been spoken to him and he believed it. We're told in verse 39 that the Ethiopian goes away rejoicing. This was a true conversion. *How can you be sure you've really trusted Christ, and repented, like Peter says to do? How do you know you're not among those who only* think *they know Jesus?*

Read 9:1–9

Observe

Where does Saul want to go, and why?

What stops Saul on the way? What does Jesus ask Saul, and then what does He ask Saul to do?

What happens to Saul as a result of this confrontation?

Interpret

Jesus tells Saul that Saul is persecuting Him. Saul never actually met Jesus. Why would Jesus say this to him?

Apply

At this point, let's take a close look at who Saul is:

- Named after first king of Israel
- Becomes an Apostle
- Highly educated, by Gamaliel in Jerusalem
- Became a Pharisee
- Was a Roman citizen (inherited from his dad)

There were many *Christians* in the early church, as we have seen, but only a few apostles. This is because in order to be an apostle, you had to have seen Jesus, among other things. This is how Saul (Paul) became an apostle. Even though he never saw Jesus while he was alive, he was allowed to become an apostle because he saw Jesus here, in the passage we just read.

Saul was heading for Damascus to persecute more Christians. He was really a go-getter! Saul was a rising star among the Pharisees; young and ambitious, he had his mind set to be as successful as possible, and he was making it happen . . . that is until Christ stopped him in his tracks. This may be one of the most important conversions in the history of Christianity, as we'll see through the rest of Acts.

Saul's fatal mistake was not realizing who he was persecuting. He made an error of judgment in assuming he was persecuting people who were against the God of Israel. In reality Saul was persecuting Jesus Himself! It should comfort you to know that Jesus empathizes with you (if you've trusted Him as your savior) so much that when *you* go through trials and hardships, it's as though it is actually *him* going through those trials. Take a moment to thanks God for allowing you to be one of his children.

Read 9:10–22

Observe

Why did Saul travel to Tarsus (v. 13–14)?

What did he actually end up doing once he got there?

What does Christ tell Ananias Saul will do (vs. 15–16)?

What is the first thing Saul does after his vision is cured?

Interpret

Why was Saul a good candidate for the role God had chosen for him to play in the spread of Christianity, described in verses 15–16?

Read verses 1 and 2 of chapter 9. Now read verses 21-22. Describe the change that has taken place in Saul's life in just 20 verses:

Apply

Saul went to Damascus specifically to throw Christians in jail. Christianity was new, and the spread of Christianity was threatening the iron grip of Judaism in the Jewish world. In this chapter, Saul goes from being the frontrunner of Christian persecution, to being the most outspoken Christian in the world! What an amazing testimony of the power Christ can have in a life. We're told in verse 20, "At once he began to preach in the synagogues that Jesus is the Son of God." This was a 180 degree turn-around from how Saul used to live! He's now going in the complete opposite direction; God had opened his eyes not just physically (v. 18), but spiritually-speaking as well. *Does your life look to others and to yourself completely different than it would look if you had never trusted Christ as your savior? This week, what is God challenging you to do differently in order to show a real change in your life? Write that area below:*

Read 9:23–31

Observe

Saul has to escape Damascus and go to Jerusalem.
Why does he do this?

How do the apostles in Jerusalem respond to Saul at first?

Who goes to bat for Saul (defends him)? How does this
person defend him?

Interpret

Read Galatians 1:13–23 and answer the following questions:

Verses 18–20 refer to the passage we just read in Acts, about Saul
going to Jerusalem. So, how long was Saul in Jerusalem, according
to this passage?

Have you read this passage carefully? This is where Paul personally tells his testimony. In verse 16, what does he say his job from God is?

Apply

So now the change is complete, and the Jews are actually trying to kill Saul for preaching about Jesus! What a great testimony to the truth of Christianity; the one who was the leading persecutor (as we saw in Gal 1:13-23) is now the leading defender of the faith.

Read verse 31 one more time. Now that Saul is a Christian, there is a time of peace. But notice what happens to the church: it is "strengthened," "encouraged," "growing." Why? The key is the last phrase; the Christians are "living in the fear of the Lord." With everything the new Christians could fear (physical torture, death, being shunned by friends or society), they chose to fear God. We sometimes tend to fear other things more than God our creator. It's easy to get caught up in fearing people's opinion of you, or that you won't make the basketball, track, or volleyball team. That you'll be made fun of for stepping out and changing something in your life. Clear away all these misplaced fears, and fear God's opinion. Fear his commands. *Below, list a few things you sometimes get caught up in "fearing." Determine this week to make fear of God your number one priority.*

Read 9:32–43

Observe

Going back to the map you used last week, find the towns of Lydda and Joppa, and circle them.

Using the scale on the map, about how many miles apart are these two towns?

How long had Aeneas been bedridden? Why was he bedridden?

Interpret

Why do you think the women mourned the death of Dorcas, in verse 39? Why did they take it so hard?

Look back at and read one of our key verses for this study, Acts 1:8. You'll notice that at this point in Acts, the disciples are fulfilling Jesus' words by being His disciples in Judea. In Acts 1:8, what does Jesus promise will happen to the disciples before they go out witnessing for Him?

How does that relate to the two stories you just read today (about Aeneas and Dorcas)?

What is the result of each of these miracles (vv. 35 and 43)?

Apply

In Acts 1:8, Jesus promises to give the disciples power (through the Holy Spirit), in order for them to be powerful witnesses. As a result, they are able to perform miracles like what we just read about. Notice that Aeneas had been bedridden for 8 years! Can you imagine lying in bed for 8 years? The man was paralyzed. Peter truly showed the power of God when he commanded Aeneas to walk. "Immediately" (v. 34) Aeneas got up and walked on legs that hadn't touched the ground in 8 years! As a result of both miracles, the people believed in Christ.

Take a moment to look back at the story of Dorcas (especially verses 36 and 39. *What kind of woman was Dorcas? How does the description of Dorcas challenge you, and how might you apply her example to your life this week?*

Read 10:1–23

Observe

Describe Cornelius.

Was he a Jew or a non-Jew?

Cornelius, the Centurion, lived in Caesarea. Find and circle this city on the map. (You may see it as "Caesarea Maritima")

Both Peter and Cornelius see a vision in this chapter. Below, describe the vision Peter sees.

Interpret

Turn to the Old Testament book of Leviticus and read 11:26–31, and 11:41–45. What do these verses have to do with what Peter says in Acts 10:14?

Apply

Chapter 10 is the final chapter that concerns the "Judea and Samaria" portion of Acts 1:8. After this, we move on to the "ends of the earth." Before doing that, however, God needs to relay a very important message to Peter, who so involved in spreading the gospel. Did you pick up on what that message is, from today's passage?

From Leviticus 11, you probably noticed that there were a lot of animals the Jews were not allowed to eat. These were called "unclean" animals. No Jew would ever eat or touch the carcass of one of these animals. However, God commands Peter in a vision to "kill and eat" a group of animals, some of which were unclean (it's no coincidence that Peter is "very hungry" (v. 10) when he sees the vision). God has declared many of the "unclean" animals as now being "clean." But is this really about what Peter is allowed to eat?

We'll see tomorrow how Peter's vision has to do with who the Gospel is open to. Before we get to that point, *are there people you believe are exempt from becoming Christians? Is there ever a person of whom God would say, "they're 'unclean' and not worthy of becoming one of My children"*?

Read 10:24–48

Observe

What did Peter find when he arrived at Cornelius's house in Caesarea (vv. 24 and 27).

Were the people Jews or Gentiles?

What is Peter doing here that is unusual?

Interpret

Do you think Peter had been strict in keeping the Jewish laws (like we read about yesterday in Lev 11), or did he look at them more like suggestions?

Recalling Peter's dream of God telling him it was now okay to eat unclean animals, what do you think that dream has to do with what we read today? What was God communicating to Peter? (see v. 34)

Apply

The Jewish mindset towards "Gentiles" (or non-Jews) was that they were unclean or profane, just like the animals in Leviticus 11 were unclean. This is an extremely important chapter in Acts, because God reveals that He's changing the way he wants to spread belief in Him.

Peter, a Jew, does something taboo by visiting and eating with Gentiles. But he does this because God told him it was ok. Not only that, but we see that it was God's will that the Gentiles be reached with the Gospel. In fact, at the end of this chapter, the Gentiles with Cornelius (there was a large group of family and friends with him (v. 27), were filled with the Holy Spirit, just like some of the Jews on the day of Pentecost! God was really showing Peter that there was no difference between Jew and non-Jew.

As non-Jewish Christians, we're like Cornelius. Though non-Jews could be saved before this, Acts 10 marks the beginning of a real effort to reach non-Jews with the Gospel. *According to verse 34, "God does not show favoritism." Below, write what you think that means, and how it should affect your sharing your faith with others.*

Read 11:1–18

Observe

Why are the "circumcised believers" (Jewish men) angry at Peter when he goes back to Jerusalem?

Below, in your own words, explain how Peter defends himself:

Interpret

In verse 15, Peter says "the Holy Spirit came on them as he had come on us at the beginning." Who is Peter saying the Holy Spirit came to? Look back in chapter 10 and write the verse where this actually happens.

And, what does Peter mean by "the beginning" in verse 15?

Read verse 18. What do you think really convinced the Jews that salvation was now available to the Gentiles?

Apply

If there's a warm fuzzy passage in the book of Acts, this is it. Here, the Jewish men in Jerusalem heard through the grapevine that Peter had gone to the house of a Gentile and eaten with him and others. It outraged the Jews that Peter, such a strong figure in Judaism, had done such a thing. Before you're too hard on these Jerusalem Jews, you need to realize what a radical thing Peter had done. Eating with a Gentile was very much taboo, and Peter only did such a thing because he had a direct command from God (10:15).

What makes this such a neat passage is the Jews' response at the end: instead of treating Peter like an outcast who has denied the faith, they praised God that He's opened salvation to the Gentiles! The MacArthur Study Bible says that this is "one of the most shocking admissions in Jewish history." God was truly working in amazing ways, both with the Gentiles *and* the Jews. *Have you forgotten what a privilege it is to know Christ as your savior? If you've been forgiven of your sins, take a moment today and thank God that He loved you enough to make salvation available to you.*

Read 11:19–30

Observe

The author here mentions "those who had been scattered by the persecution in connection with Stephen." What persecution is this referring to?

Did the people who went to Antioch only preach to Jews there, or to the Gentiles as well?

According to this passage, what did people call the believers in Antioch (this is the first time they were referred to by this name)?

Interpret

The stoning of Stephen was a shocking and profound event for those in Jerusalem who believed in Jesus. Can you see any positive side to the stoning? Do you see any ways God used that event?

Read verse 26. What does "Christian" mean, and why do you think the disciples were called that?

Here we're introduced to an important person: Barnabas. Using verses 22–26, describe Barnabas, mentioning the kind of person he was and the kinds of things he did.

Apply

Did you know that "Christian" literally means "little Christ?" The believers in Antioch (which is south of modern-day Turkey), were called "little Christs" because their behavior reminded people of Jesus. They didn't call themselves "Christians," but others in the outside world gave them that name.

If nobody knew you went to church or considered yourself a "Christian," would they know you're a believer in Christ by your actions and words alone? *What is one thing you can change this week that might be keeping people from recognizing you as a "little Christ?" Write that one thing below.*

Read 12:1–17

Observe

Who did Herod have killed?

Who did he seize next, and why?

How many soldiers were guarding Peter?

Interpret

Read this passage again carefully. Write two questions that come to your mind after reading this:

If someone were to suggest to you that what happens in this passage is impossible, and could not have happened, how would you respond?

Apply

As amazing as this story is, there is another story going on in verses 1–4. Why does Herod have Peter seized and thrown in prison? Because he saw that the killing of James pleased the Jews. The Jews didn't like these radical Christians and liked seeing them killed. Also, Herod Agrippa (AD 37–44), had a rocky relationship with his homeland, Rome, who had put him in power in Israel (at this time, Rome was occupying Israel as a foreign power). Since things weren't going well with Rome, Herod tried to build support for himself among the Jews.

In the midst of this amazing story about Peter, what a sad story is the life of Herod Agrippa! He tried so hard to win the Jews' favor; he was a sell-out, doing whatever made others happy. And he only reigned for eight years. He spent his brief time on earth winning man's favor instead of God's, and even though he lived in luxury compared to the Christians, his time of comfort here on earth was very brief. *What about you? Are you living to please God or the people around you? Can you think of something in your life that you do to please your friends, that God would have you not do?*

Read 12:17–25

Observe

What happened to the men who were guarding Peter?

Find Tyre and Sidon on the map from two weeks ago.

Interpret

Why do you think Tyre and Sidon were important cities?

Why did God strike down Herod? Do you think God's judgment on Herod was too harsh? Why or why not?

Apply

Have you ever heard of Josephus? He isn't in the Bible, but Josephus is a First Century Jewish historian, who recorded a lot of information that's helpful to us. Obviously, his writings aren't inspired, as the Bible is, so unlike the Bible, they may contain some inaccuracies. We can use the information from Josephus as an aid to understanding more of what we read in the Scripture; but the Bible is always our ultimate authority.

Josephus gives us an interesting bit of information about this scene. He tells us that Herod wore a garment made of silver. The picture I get of Herod is of a self-conscious, unstable man, looking for the praise of others, while at the same time being very unsure of himself. Where does he go wrong in this passage? When he lets people call him a god, of course! When the people told him he sounded like a god, he should have silenced the people and told them he was only a man. His response, in fact, should have been more like what Peter would have done. Go back to *Acts 10:24–25 Below, summarize how Peter responded to praise, and how that is different from how Herod responded. Then, consider how his week, how can you be more like Peter when it comes to bringing God praise?*

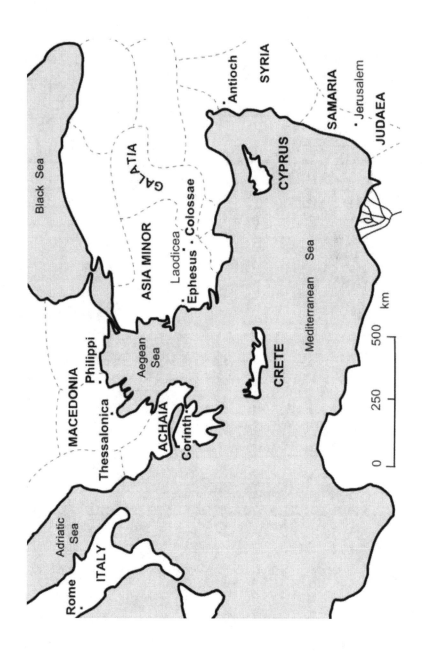

Read 13:1–12

Observe

The "Holy Spirit" is mentioned very often in the book of Acts. The Spirit is mentioned three times in this passage. Next to each number, write the verses that reference the Holy Spirit. Then, next to the reference, describe what the Holy Spirit did in those verses:

1)

2)

3)

Interpret

Looking at the things the Holy Spirit did in this passage, have you ever witnessed the Holy Spirit do things like this?

Do you think the Holy Spirit is doing the same things today that took place back in the early First Century? If so, what are some examples? If not, why do you think there has been a change in what the Holy Spirit is doing?

Apply

Did you notice what Paul did as soon as they arrived in Cyprus? He went to the synagogues, where the Jews would have been. This will become a pattern with Paul; he always goes to the Jews first. Paul, of course, was a Jew, and he had an open door with the Jews; he had credibility with them, and they would pay attention to what he said. *Are there any people God has placed in your life because you have some connection to them? Is there a way you can use the things you have in common to talk with them about what you believe?*

The Holy Spirit does some interesting things in this passage. Continue to pay attention to what the Spirit does. Acts is about the "acts" of the disciples, but it is also about the "acts" of the Holy Spirit. We'll learn more about this as we study.

Read 13:13–31

Observe

What is the first thing that Paul and his companions did when they went to Antioch?

List the main points of what Paul shares in verses 17–31.

Interpret

Why do you think Paul chooses to share the information he does? Why not just tell these people about Jesus?

Do verses 27–29 reveal anything about how God operates? If so, what?

Apply

Instead of just walking into the synagogue (which Paul always does first upon entering a city) and telling the people about Jesus, Paul chooses to begin by reviewing the history of Israel, which is recorded in the Old Testament. Why would he do it this way? One reason might be to establish rapport with the Jews he's speaking to. He's showing them he can be trusted, that he knows Israel's history. Paul was actually a very devout Jew before he became a Christian. He also may want to show that the life and death of Jesus were predicted in the Old Testament, and show that the Old Testament and Jesus are not two different religions, but that Christ came to fulfill the Old Testament. He presents Jesus as the next step in the Jewish story, and he's pleading with these Jews not to miss this step and stay stuck in a rut! This continues to be an issue for Jews today, many of whom don't see Jesus as fulfilling the Old Testament prophecies. What did you find out about verses 27-29? Read them again. God uses wicked people, and sin, to accomplish his purposes. This doesn't mean he condones sin, but it does mean that ultimately it results in His will. *Are there difficult people or circumstances in your life this week that God may use to work out His will in your life?*

Read 13:32–43

Observe

Read verses 32–33 again. According to this verse, what did God do to fulfill His promises to "our fathers" (Old Testament Jews)?

Interpret

There are many promises God made to the Jews in the Old Testament concerning Jesus and His life and death. Many of these promises are in the books of prophecy. Some are in Psalms as well. Read Psalm 22 and think of it as a prophecy about the manner of Jesus' death. Below, write down as many things as you can from that Psalm that remind you of Jesus' death:

Apply

Do not leave this passage behind without catching Paul's main point, as he speaks here in the Jewish synagogue on the Sabbath. I believe his main point is found in verses 38–39. Read these verses again.

In verse 39, Paul explains to the Jews that the Law of Moses (first 5 books of Old Testament) could not justify them from sins. Nobody could have possibly kept the entire law perfectly! It was impossible. In his speech, Paul is explaining that the purpose of the Law was to point them to Jesus, and that's why he's telling them about Jesus now. He doesn't want the Jews to keep serving the law. Jesus came to do one thing: bring forgiveness of sins (v. 38).

Think about that! All 33 years Jesus spent on earth were directed towards one goal: making it possible for you to be forgiven of your sins, by trusting Jesus as your savior. For the Old Testament Jews, obeying the law wasn't good enough. For you, being a good person isn't good enough . . . even if you're *really* good! There's only one way to heaven, and that's by asking Christ to forgive you of your sins and trusting his sacrifice alone as sufficient payment for your sins. Have you done that? If not, you need to! If you are a Christian, have you begun to take Jesus' sacrifice for granted? Take a moment today and thank God that he sent Jesus to be a sacrifice for your sins.

Read 13:44–52

Observe

Why did the Jews speak abusively to Paul and Barnabas?

How did the Gentiles respond to Paul's message?

What did the Jews do when the Word of God began to spread as a result of Paul's message?

Interpret

Turn to and read the following passages, and explain what each of them has in common:

Luke 4:28–29

Luke 11:53–54

Matthew 21:45-46

Finally, what do these passages have to do with verses 44-45 that we read today from Acts?

Apply

Much can be learned from the passage we read today, but one of the most important things to learn is about human nature. You probably noticed that the Jews responded to Jesus *just like they responded to Paul and Barnabas in this chapter.* Here in Acts, the issue is that Paul and Barnabas are getting a big following: almost the whole city had come out to hear them (v. 44). That's a lot of people! And of course, the Jews were jealous of that popularity, because *they* were supposed to be the religious elite, the ones the people went to.

In addition to revealing how powerful jealousy can be (jealousy ultimately caused the Jews to call for Jesus' crucifixion), it also reveals how resistant people can be to the truth. We see that very often in our own culture as well; people may know the truth but try very hard to convince themselves otherwise. You may have noticed that in non-Christians you know.

If you've found yourself ridiculed or looked down in because you go to church or people know you're a Christian, be glad about that! Paul and Barnabas were treated the same way.

Read 14:1–7

Observe

Paul and Barnabas have now gone from Antioch to Paphos to Perga to a different Antioch (there are two) and now to Iconium. Look in the back of your Bible and see if you have a map showing Paul's Missionary Journeys. If so, look at this first journey. It's a good idea to look at where Paul went on these journeys. He was the first to bring the Gospel to these cities. What he was saying had never been heard.

By now you've probably noticed what Paul immediately does when he first enters a city. Look at verse 1: What is it that he always does?

Why did God enable them to do signs and wonders (v. 3)?

Describe the response of the people in Iconium.

Interpret

Why do you think some chose to believe while others did not?

Why do some of the Jews react negatively to Paul and Barnabas's message?

Apply

Several years ago a book called *The DaVinci Code* became a national sensation. It was a work of fiction that caused many to assume that Jesus had a wife and children. This even led to someone "discovering" the tomb of Jesus and His family. I don't know about you, but when I read about these things, sometimes I feel discouraged about how the truth can become so badly mangled. When we look at this passage from Acts, we find that this has been going on since the first few years the Gospel was ever preached. The phrase Luke chooses here—"poisoned their minds"—is very descriptive, and applies to our own day as well. *If you've been discouraged lately, take heart in the fact that God's work is still going on, just like it continued in Iconium under such heavy opposition. Be one of the ones who stand for and proclaim the truth, as Paul and Barnabas did.*

Read 14:8–20

Observe

How long had the lame man from Lystra been crippled?

What enables Him to be healed?

How do the people in Lystra react to this? Are Jews or non-Jews?

Interpret

In verses 1517, while trying to tell the people they are not the gods Zeus and Hermes, Paul also shares the gospel with the Lystra people. How is this similar to or different from how he proclaims the gospel to the Jews in 13:16–41?

What can you learn from this about sharing the gospel?

Amazingly, in verses 19-20, the people stone Paul, whom they had just tried to honor as the god Zeus! Why do you think the people had such a change in heart?

Apply

Are you noticing any patterns as we read through Acts? As Paul continues to travel from city to city and begins by preaching in the synagogue each time, there is something else that continually happens as well: he is constantly persecuted and driven out by the Jews. Ironically, Paul had been doing this to Christians as well, before he "saw the light" back in chapter 9. In this chapter, the Greek people are amazed by the healing of the lame man (who had never walked!), and they try to honor Paul and Barnabas as gods. That alone speaks for how authentic the miracles were. Maybe you've seen or heard of a healing service, where a preacher touches someone's head and they fall backwards, cured of a headache or poor vision. This does not compare that to what Paul does here and in other places. Paul puts a man on his feet who has never walked a day in his life. What an amazing moment for this man.

Just like God changed this crippled man's life, if you're a Christian He's changed your life too. Think of how God has transformed your life and take a moment today to pray and thank God for the good He has done for you.

Read 14:21–28

Observe

Why did they return to Lystra, Iconium, and Antioch?

How did they encourage the believers?

Where does their journey end?

Interpret

Why was Paul especially qualified to tell the people, "We must go through many hardships to enter the kingdom of God."?

This is the end of the first missionary journey. What did Paul set out to do on this journey? In your opinion, did he accomplish that?

Apply

We come across a very important lesson in this passage about faith. Instead of just leaving the new Christians in the dust, Paul and Barnabas travel back to the cities they had visited, "strengthening the disciples and encouraging them to remain true to the faith." Paul also wrote many letters, known as the epistles, for that same reason. Paul was in the business of making disciples, not just making people who made a one-time decision. Paul knew faith can waver, and he didn't want the new Christians to abandon their faith. He went back to strengthen it.

Has your faith ever faltered? Do you sometimes have doubts about what you believe? If so, you're not alone! In the book *Mere Christianity*, C.S. Lewis points out that oftentimes, it's not *reasons* that make us falter in our faith, but *worries, trials, temptation, peer pressure*. These things don't argue against Christianity so much as they raise the stakes, and sometimes put our true faith to the test. So Lewis give a good explanation of what faith means in our lives: "Now faith . . . is the art of holding on to things your *reason* has once accepted, in spite of your changing moods."

Do you ever wonder where faith comes into your life? It's when you're tempted to give up on what you believe because it doesn't seem true at the moment. As Lewis concludes, "We have to be continually reminded of what we believe." And that's why Paul traveled back to the cities to visit the new Christians. You also have to be continually reminded, in order for your faith to remain strong. *This week, how can you be in the habit of reminding yourself what you believe?*

Read 15:1–11

Observe

What do the Jews (they are called "Judaizers") from Judea say the new Christians must do to be saved? How do Paul and Barnabas respond?

What do Paul and Barnabas do as they travel to Jerusalem?

Interpret

Read the statement the Pharisees make in verse 5. Peter responds to this idea in verses 7–11. Below, summarize what Peter says to the Jews:

Who do you think Peter is referring to in verses 7–9? (Hint: see chapter 10.)

Apply

Some of the Jews continue to cause problems as the gospel spreads throughout the Mediterranean world. What do they do this time? They suggest that the Gentiles Paul had been winning for Christ were actually not saved, because they had not been circumcised (if necessary, look this word up in dictionary). Circumcision was part of Old Testament law. God required every baby boy, at eight days old, to be circumcised. Of course, this wasn't the only thing the law required; there were hundreds of other things the Jews had to observe. The Judaizers, however, focused on this one thing.

Did you notice what Paul and Barnabas do on their way to confront these Jews? They stop at various cities, telling the Christians how many of the Gentiles had been saved. Do Paul and Barnabas seem like men who aren't sure about the issue of Gentiles being saved? No; they're confident that circumcision isn't a part of salvation.

Peters words to the Jews help us as Christians be confident that salvation is by grace, through faith. Just like the Gentiles didn't have to be circumcised to be Christians, we (as non-Jews) don't need to do good works to get into heaven. We simply put our faith in Christ, as verse 11 says: "No! We believe it is through the grace of our Lord Jesus that we are saved, just as they are." *Is your faith in Christ for salvation, or in yourself?*

Read 15:12–21

Observe

What does James say Simon described?

How does the quote from Amos (vv. 16–18) prove this?

What is James's point (v. 19)?

What does James say the new Gentile Christians should abstain from?

Interpret

Why does James mention what he does in verse 21? This is a tough one. Think hard!

Apply

This passage is about loving your brothers and sister in Christ. You may be thinking, "How do you come to that conclusion?" Let's take a closer look . . .

Remember what's going on in this chapter. Some Jews (called Judaizers), had gone to the new Gentile (non-Jewish) Christians Paul had led to Christ. The Judaizers told them they had to be circumcised or they couldn't be saved. In his speech here, James uses a passage from the Old Testament (vs. 16-18), to show that God's plan was to save Gentiles and that they didn't have to become Jews before becoming Christians!

However, there are a few things James says they should refrain from. Read verse 20 again. These things all have to do with idol worship (even sexual immorality). They were also forbidden in the Old Testament Law. Verse 21 mentions that the Law of Moses was preached "in every city" to point out that, since everyone is still hearing that there are certain foods Jews aren't to eat, that even new Gentile Christians should avoid those things. James was afraid that Jews might see Gentiles doing certain things (for example, eating meat that had been sacrificed to idols), and do the same thing. This might cause them to do something that went against what their conscience told them to do, even though it may not have been a sin for the Gentiles.

Are there things you might be saying or doing that may cause a brother or sister in Christ to stumble spiritually? Be careful what you say or do; others may be watching.

Read 15:22–35

Observe

Why did a letter need to be sent to the Gentile believers in Antioch, Syria, and Cilicia?

Why did Judas and Silas come along with the letter?

Interpret

Verse 31 says that when the letter was read to the people in the church in Antioch, they were "glad for its encouraging message." What do you think it was about the message that made them glad?

Apply

Remember, some of the new Gentile Christians had been told that they needed to keep some of the Jewish law's requirements in order to truly be saved. Specifically, they were told they needed to be circumcised. In other words, they were told that faith in Christ was *not* enough for salvation!

Verses 24–28 record what the letter said that Judas and Silas brought to Antioch. What probably encouraged the people so much was that they were told that faith *is* enough for salvation, and they didn't need to live by Jewish (Old Testament) law. The letter does mention a few things they were supposed to do, which we read about earlier in the chapter—they're recorded in verse 29, and are part of Jewish law. But as we learned last study, they were supposed to avoid these things for the sake of not causing the Jewish Christians to stumble spiritually.

What was so encouraging about this letter? It lifted a huge burden off their shoulders! Imagine if somebody told you that in order to be saved, you had to undergo torture, or obey a huge list of rules. The Christians in Antioch were relieved to find out that all they had to do was have faith in Christ. The same is true of you. Take a moment today to thank God for saving you—by faith, and not works.

Read 15:36–41

Observe

What was Paul's complaint about John Mark?

What is the result of the disagreement between Barnabas and Paul?

Why do Paul and Silas go through Syria and Cilicia (v. 41)?

Interpret

Why do you think John Mark's leaving them was such a big deal to Paul? (For the actual occurrence of this, see Acts 13:13 and the context there.)

Paul mentions John Mark in 2 Timothy 4:11, which was written some time after our passage from Acts. Read 2 Tim 4:11. What does Paul say about John Mark?

How has Paul's opinion of John seem to have changed?

Apply

The story of the relationship between Paul and John Mark is a success story. Obviously, Paul was very upset with John for deserting them—Acts 15:39 says Paul and Barnabas had a "sharp disagreement" over the issue of whether or not to bring John Mark along. But notice what Paul himself says of John later on, in 2 Timothy 4:11. Paul says he is "helpful" to his ministry.

Paul and John Mark had resolved their differences, so that they could minister for God together. How often do broken relationships between Christians hinder them from serving God? Far too often! It's awesome to see that Paul and John resolved restored their relationship. But it's sad to think of how Satan sometimes causes fights between Christians, who end up focusing on themselves instead of serving God. *Is there someone in your life you need to reach out to, in order to restore the relationship? Show your spiritual maturity by getting things right, like Paul and John Mark did.*

Read 16:1–15

Observe

What makes Timothy somewhat unusual (v. 1)?

How is Lydia described as responding to Paul's message (v. 14)?

What does Lydia do right after this?

Interpret

Can you think of any benefits to Timothy being part Jewish and part Greek?

Apply

This is the beginning of Paul's second missionary journey. In going from Troas to Neapolis, Paul and his companions were taking the gospel from Asia to Europe; Troas is in modern-day Turkey, and Neapolis is in Greece. Notice that, for the first time, in verse 10 the author uses the word "we." Read this verse again. This indicates that now the author, Luke, is also traveling with Paul, Silas, and Timothy.

Timothy's mother was Jewish and his father was Greek. Paul made sure Timothy was circumcised. As we learned before, that wasn't part of Timothy becoming a Christian. However, it did communicate to the Jews his commitment to the Jewish God. It wasn't a requirement for salvation, but it helped his testimony.

Since Timothy was part Jew and part Greek, he had the unique ability to reach out to both cultures. You see, God chose Timothy for a very specific reason, just like He chose Paul and the others for different reasons. God uses many different sorts of people to get the job done, and He chose Timothy partly because of who he could preach. *Think of who you are as a person; your background, interests, and personality. God chose you for a reason too! Who can you reach for Jesus that others might not be able to? God made you who you are for a reason!*

Read 16:1–15

Observe

What makes Timothy somewhat unusual (v. 1)

How is Lydia described as responding to Paul's message (v. 14)?

What does Lydia do right after this?

Interpret

Can you think of any benefits to Timothy being part Jewish and part Greek?

Apply

This is the beginning of Paul's second missionary journey. In going from Troas to Neapolis, Paul and his companions were taking the gospel from Asia to Europe; Troas is in modern-day Turkey, and Neapolis is in Greece. Notice that, for the first time, in verse 10 the author uses the word "we." Read this verse again. This indicates that now the author, Luke, is also traveling with Paul, Silas, and Timothy.

Timothy's mother was Jewish and his father was Greek. Paul made sure Timothy was circumcised. As we learned before, that wasn't part of Timothy becoming a Christian. However, it did communicate to the Jews his commitment to the Jewish God. It wasn't a requirement for salvation, but it helped his testimony.

Since Timothy was part Jew and part Greek, he had the unique ability to reach out to both cultures. You see, God chose Timothy for a very specific reason, just like He chose Paul and the others for different reasons. God uses many different sorts of people to get the job done, and He chose Timothy partly because of who he could reach. *Think of who you are as a person; your background, interests, and personality. God chose you for a reason too! Who can you reach for Jesus that others might not be able to? God made you who you are for a reason!*

Read 16:16–24

Observe

What was this slave girl doing that was earning her owners a profit?

What did Paul do as a result? Why were the girl's owners upset by this?

What were Paul and Silas accused of, and what was their punishment?

Interpret

Why do you think that what the girl was doing was an annoyance to Paul and the others?

How do you think Paul was able to cast the spirit out of the girl (Mark 3:15)? Do all Christians have this ability?

Why do you think God allowed this horrible thing to happen to Paul and Silas?

Apply

Imagine for a moment that you're driving to a town a few hours away. On the way, you stop for gas, and while you're there you do something to offend one of the residents. As a result, you're dragged to the town square, beaten with rods, and chained in jail. Would the though, *why would God let this happen* cross your mind?

This is exactly what happened to Paul and Silas. Their beating was severe, and their feet were put in stocks (v. 24); a practice reserved for the more dangerous criminals, their legs would have been spread apart uncomfortably and fastened down. How often do we get discouraged, or even question our faith, as a result of much smaller problems? We'll leave Paul and Silas chained for the moment. There was a purpose for what they were going through, but like Paul and Silas, we haven't found out yet what it is. For today, let their response be a challenge to you: *the next time you face a tough time and wonder why God is allowing it, remember that God put Paul and Silas through even tougher times—and He had a purpose behind it.*

Read 16:25–34

Observe

What were Paul and Silas doing while they were chained in prison?

What is the jailer about to do before Paul stops him?

Describe how the jailer responds to what Paul says in verse 31. Include each thing the jailer does, and his attitude.

Interpret

At this point in the chapter (consider what has taken place), are you surprised that Paul and Silas are praying and singing hymns to God? Why or why not?

What do you think causes the jailer to ask what he does in verse 30: "Sirs, what must I do to be saved."?

Apply

Can you believe Paul and Silas were singing and praising God, at midnight, while they were in prison? They had just been "severely flogged" (v.23) for no good reason. We're told the other prisoners are listening to them (v. 25). What an amazing testimony! These two guys had no fear of man in them; it was completely overcome with fear for and love of God. *Are you outspoken when it comes to your faith and trust in Christ, or do you try to hide it?*

Paul and Silas must have wondered why God allowed them to be unjustly beaten and placed in prison. Here, maybe their question had been answered. The Philippian jailer and his whole household trust in Jesus as a result of Paul and Silas's testimony. You see, there was something undeniably different about these two missionaries that people just couldn't ignore. *Do people notice any difference in your life because you're a Christian? If not, what do you plan to do this week to change?*

Read 16:35–40

Observe

How does Paul respond when the Philippian jailer tells him that he (Paul) and Silas are being released?

What's the last thing Paul and Silas do before they leave Philippi?

Interpret

Why do you think the magistrates decided to release Paul and Silas from prison?

Now that we're at the end of chapter 16, think back to what has happened, particularly in Philippi. Below, describe what you think the general opinion of Christians was in the city of Philippi, following this episode:

Apply

As you considered the last question, did the words "trouble-makers" come to your mind? It might have appeared to some in Philippi that Christians were fanatics who just liked stirring up trouble. But consider why they were arrested in the first place: Paul cast a demon out of a young lady! Is that really grounds to be thrown in prison? Just like Jesus, these Christians' only fault was that they had done good for others. If you face trials and difficulties in your day-to-day life, let it be because you're committed to Christ, regardless of how people view you as a result, and you're doing good for others. *What good can you to tomorrow as evidence that you're a Christian?*

Read 17:1–9

Observe

If you have a map in the back of your Bible, locate Thessalonica, in Greece. Notice that this is farther than Paul has ever spread the gospel.

What was Paul's purpose for going to the synagogue in Thessalonica?

How did the Jews respond to Paul's preaching?

When the Jews bring Jason before the city officials, what do they accuse Paul and the others of doing?

Interpret

Why do you think the Jews were jealous when they heard Paul's preaching?

How would you have felt if you were Jason, in this story?

Apply

On what grounds did the Jews arrest Jason and accuse Paul and the others? As the MacArthur Bible Commentary mentions, "One of the most serious crimes in the Roman Empire was to acknowledge allegiance to any king but Caesar. Did the Jews really care about whether or not Caesar was being honored? Of course not! They were using any leverage they could find to have the Christians arrested and persecuted.

What would motivate them to do this? As the Jews mention in verse 6, the Christians were "causing trouble all over the world." That means Paul's message was having a wide influence. The Jews from the synagogues were supposed to be the religious "big shots." They were too proud to admit that Paul's message was right: that Christ had indeed come to earth and died for their sins. Far from accepting him, these Pharisees were caught up in protecting their jobs and their reputations.

What about you? Does your pride ever cause you treat others unfairly? Those who accepted Christ in Acts humbly recognized that Christ had come to save them from their sins. This week, let humility characterize your relationships with others.

Read 17:10–15

Observe

How are the Bereans described in verse 11?

How often did the Bereans "examine the Scriptures?"

Why did they do this?

What did the Jews do when they learned Paul had gone to Berea?

Interpret

Why do you think the Jews continue to try to stir up trouble for Paul?

How was Paul once similar to these Jews? Why is he different now (at this point in Acts)?

What do you think was different about the Bereans, that gave them such a desire to understand the Scriptures for themselves?

Apply

The description of the Bereans in verse 11 is very famous. In some ways, it forms the foundation of why we do this Bible study. Like the Bereans, we want to be a people who are searching the Scriptures, *every day*, for ourselves, and not just being spoon fed once or twice per week. We're told by Luke that this quality makes the Bereans of a "mor noble" character than the Thessalonians.

Are you cultivating a desire for spiritual understanding in your life? It won't come automatically. Your desire grows for whatever you feed it. Feeding it entertainment will give a greater desire for entertainment. Feeding it gossip will yield a stronger desire for more gossip. Seeking wisdom will give you a greater desire for more wisdom. Today, determine to be like the "noble" Bereans. Cultivate a desire for the Word. Seek answers to the questions you have, or the questions people ask of you that may cause you to doubt. Don't be an empty body! Use your head, ask tough questions, and become one of the few truth-seekers.

Read 17:15–21

Observe

While in Athens, what does Paul see that distresses him?

Why do they think Paul is preaching a foreign god?

What do the men who meet at the Areopagus spend all their time doing?

Interpret

Paul is distressed to see all the idols in Athens. What "idols" do people worship in our own day and age? List some below:

Up to this point, how is the response of the Athenians different from the response Paul has received in other cities he's traveled to in the book of Acts?

We're confronted here with two new terms. In a dictionary, Bible dictionary, or online, look up the definitions of these words, which describe Greeks two different belief systems:

Epicureanism:

Stoicism:

Apply

We won't find out until next study what Paul has to say to these philosophers. They spend *all* their time talking about and listening to the latest ideas! Doesn't that sound like a nice career? Note that they're good listeners; at least they want to hear Paul out. Christianity is brand new, and they have no bias against the truth Paul is hoping to convey.

One way Athens is similar to our own culture is in verse 16. Paul is distressed because the people have so many idols. Their lives are devoted to a lie! You may not see Americans bow and worship idols . . . but we have them too. *Are there things in your life you give more time, attention and worship than God? What actions do you need to take this week to change that?*

Read 17:22-34

Observe

What does Paul notice that really catches his attention?

As we saw last study, the Athenians think Paul is "advocating a foreign god" (v. 18). Now we see why. From verse 24-26, list three ways the God Paul is presenting is different from the idols the Athenians worship.

What "ignorance" did God previously overlook, which He now does not overlook, according to verse 30? Why is this true?

Interpret ...

At the beginning of this passage, Paul finds a great way to begin witnessing to the Athenians. In your own words, describe what Paul says to meet the Athenians on their own turf, and to get them listening to what he has to say:

In verses 32-34, we read of 3 different responses the people who listened to Paul had after hearing his message. Read carefully, and write down those 3 responses below:

Apply

Imagine Paul taking the message of Christianity into the heart of commerce, culture and art—Athens. It was a beautiful, thriving city . . . but it desperately needed the message Paul had to bring. This is a famous passage of Scripture. Paul uses the "UNKNOWN GOD" inscription as a springboard to begin talking to the Athenians. *What inroads could you use to gain a hearing with your friends or others who need the truth?*

You know, when you share the gospel with others, or simply share the truth, not everyone will have the same response. Some Athenians thought Paul was just an amateur philosopher (actually he was highly educated), others wanted to hear more, and others put their belief in Jesus. Our job is to share the truth, and trust God for the results.

Read 18:1–11

Observe

What was Paul's occupation (besides being a missionary)?

In verse 5, Silas and Timothy come to be with Paul. Why was this such a good thing for Paul? What seems to be the most important thing to him?

When the Jews oppose Paul (again!) how does Paul respond?

Interpret

Do you sense some frustration from Paul in verse 6? Why do you think he feels this way?

Below, describe the two different responses to the gospel; one in verse 6, and one in verse 7.

Why do you think God chose to say what he did to Paul in verses 9 and 10 at this time?

Apply

I don't know about you, but when I read what Paul said to the Jews in verse 6, I laughed out loud! Remember, every time Paul goes to a new city he—say it together, class—goes to the synagogue to preach. And *every time*, the Jews (remember, Paul himself was a leader in the Jewish religion) oppose him and drive him out of town. So what does Paul say here? Read verse 6 again, and imagine how Paul must have said this. He'd had enough of the Jews opposing him. And then what happens in the next verse? Paul goes next door and immediately the people there accept Christ.

This episode reminds us again that it's our job to tell others the truth about God. God is responsible for the results. God has to encourage Paul in verses 9 and 10 not to give up preaching. He must have been at his wits end. One final thought. In verse 6, Paul says, "Your blood be on your own head!" You see, the Jews had received the truth, and it was up to them what to do with it. The problem is, the more truth you've been given, the more responsibility you have to accept and live that truth. You'll be judged someday based on what you've done with what God's given you. *Are you being a good steward of the truth God's given you? Or is your heart hard, like the Jews were in this passage?*

Read 18:12–22

Observe

What is the Jewish complaint against Paul?

In your own words, how does Gallio, the judge, respond to their attack?

How do the people in Ephesus respond when Paul tries to leave?

Interpret

These verses conclude Paul's Second Missionary Journey. At this point, take a moment and Describe Paul, based on everything you've read up to this point. Include what you learn in this passage as well. If you had to describe him to somebody, what traits would you list? What adjectives would you use?

Apply

Gallio responds wisely to the Jews. The Greeks saw Judaism as an outside religion, and Christianity as an offshoot of that religion. Gallio realizes that the Jews are trying to use the government to settle something that is outside the role of Gallio or the government. They are frustrated that they don't get the result they want, and so they turn on and beat Sosthenes. By the way, he eventually becomes a Christian (see 1 Cor. 1:1).

So far in Acts, we haven't gotten a pretty picture of the Jews, and the end of Paul's Second Journey is no exception. They've clearly left God's law—His commandments and lifestyle He revealed to them—in the dust. The result is a people who have mistaken rules and zeal (look it up if you need to) for true Godliness. We face the same danger, if we don't make it our practice to continually seek God's truth for our lives, and to love others as Christ did. Let's make that a priority this week!

Read 18:23–28

Observe

Where was Apollos from?

What do Aquila and Priscilla do when they hear Apollos is speaking in Ephesus?

Do you think this passage suggests Apollos was doing something wrong in his preaching at Ephesus? Explain.

Interpret

Why do you think Luke might want us to know where Apollos is from?

What do you think it means that Apollos "knew only the baptism of John"?

Apply

In our passage today we see that Paul is not the only one traveling and preaching about Jesus. A man named Apollos has come to Ephesus in order to preach. This is our first introduction to Apollos, who will accompany Paul on his later journeys. Luke wants us to know some important things about Apollos. First, he is from Alexandria, Egypt. Alexandria was one of the great centers of culture and learning in the ancient world, much like New York City. If there was no status in Jesus being from Nazareth (and there wasn't) there was a lot of status in being from Alexandria. And Apollos lived up to this title. It says at the end of the passage that Apollos was able to vigorously refute his opponents in showing that Jesus was the Christ. (Remember that "Christ" is a title from the Hebrew word "anointed.") This means Apollos is showing that Jesus is the king promised in the Old Testament, the one everyone was waiting for.

Secondly, we see that Apollos, though learned, was also humble. Somehow Apollos was familiar with John's baptism but not Jesus's. He knew of John's call to repent because the Messiah had come, but did not know of the work of Christ on the cross and the resurrection. When Aquila and Priscila fill in this message for him he is not resentful or use his vigorous debate skills to prove them wrong. Instead he humbly accepts this new life-changing news and becomes a great public intellectual on behalf of the good news. Knowledge and humility; this is a powerful combination. Like Apollos, may we study hard and learn well, but may we also have the humility to listen and learn. This is how Apollos was able to help change the world.

Read 19:1–10

Observe

What are some of the things that make the baptism of John different from the baptism of Jesus (vv. 1–7). Try to list at least three:

How long does Paul preach in the synagogue? Why does he leave?

Where does Paul go after he leaves the synagogue? How long does he stay?

Interpret

Look of Romans 1:14. How does this verse relate to today's passage?

*Verse 9 says that the people in the synagogue "maligned the Way."
Paul decided to leave because they became so obstinate. Have you
ever experienced opposition from others about your Christian beliefs
or lifestyle? In what way? How did you respond?*

Apply

"The Way" is often used in Acts to describe the plan God had
revealed and accomplished to offer salvation (see 9:2). John the
Baptist offered half the story: repent from sin. But in Christ the
full "way" of salvation is revealed, answering the difficult question,
"How can God forgive?". Christ lived an impossibly perfect life in
order to die, rise again, offer salvation. This is the message Paul
brought with him to the cities of the Mediterranean.

When he arrives in Ephesus, Paul discovers that, unlike the
other cities, the Ephesians have heard about Christ already. But
when he asks if they had received the Holy Spirit, they respond that
they had not even heard of the Holy Spirit (v. 2). So Paul baptizes
them and they speak in tongues. This is the last occurrence in the
Bible of speaking in tongues (the other places are in Acts 2 and 10).

Finally, Paul's long stay in Ephesus (almost three years!)
shows how committed he was to reaching the city. In fact people
from all ooverfer the province of Asia come to hear him. When
the men in the synagogue stop listening to Paul, he leaves them.
This shows that Paul went to the Jews in the city first, but he did
not waste time when they stopped listening. Moving to the lec-
ture hall of Tyrannus was a move to a more open forum, a place
where both Jews and Gentiles could listen and debate. He stays
there two years. When it comes to the people in your life who do
not know the Lord, it may take more than a few conversations for
them to believe the gospel. Like Paul, may you be willing to form
relationships and spend the time it takes to foster deep discus-
sions about Christ.

Read 19:11–22

Observe

What do the sons of Sceva do that provokes an evil spirit?

What happens to the sons of Sceva as a result?

What is the effect of this event on the Jews and Greeks living in Ephesus?

Interpret

What causes the Jews and Greeks to hold the name of the lord "in high honor" (v. 17)?

One of the most important themes in the bible is God's sovereignty. Everything that happens–good and bad–falls under God's control. Nothing takes place that is not part of God's plan. This must mean that God uses seemingly bad things, even terrible things, for good. How do we see that in today's passage?

Apply

Verse 20 is a mantra in the book of Acts: "In this way the word of the Lord spread widely and grew in power." Different forms of this verse create seams in the book of Acts, showing major events that led to the spread of the gospel. In our passage today that event is a terrifying ordeal (see v. 16). The result is that the name of Jesus is "held in high honor" (v. 17). A demon states that he fears the name of Jesus, and knows about Paul, but has no fear of the sons of Sceva.

Demons were a reality in the first century world. In our day people don't think much about demonic activity. In *Screwtape Letters* C.S. Lewis helps us to see that in every age the demons would prefer to have people think too much about them or too little about them. The truth is that whether we see demonic activity or not, it is real. The people in Ephesus knew how real demons were, and the power of Paul, through Christ, over these demons caused the gospel to spread.

Finally, we see that when people in Ephesus believed in the gospel it had a real impact on their priorities. In verse 19 we're told that those who had practiced sorcery burned their scrolls, and that the value of these scrolls came to 50,000 drachmas. This is roughly equivalent to $4,000,000! You probably do not have any books of sorcery to burn, but has your belief in the gospel had a noticeable effect on your own priorities? Has it been costly to you to be a follower of Christ? Is there anything you feel challenged about doing as a response to God's work in your life?

Read 19:23–41

Observe

Why does Artemis start a riot in Ephesus?

What does Paul want to do during the riot in the theater?

Why do the people not listen to Alexander?

Interpret

Do you think the disciples made the right decision in stopping Paul from speaking to the crowd? What do you think he was going to say?

Why do you think Luke shares this story? Are there any ways it relates to the overall purpose of Acts?

Apply

The temple of Artemis was one of the seven wonders of the ancient world–perhaps the greatest. It measured 425 feet long by 225 feet wide, and stood over 60 feet high. It was twice the size of most Greek temples, including the Parthenon. The people of Ephesus must have been proud to be the city of Artemis. Despite this great cultural heritage, however, so many people believe Paul's message that it affects Demetrius's business. In fact Demetrius says that practically the whole province of Asia has turned to the gospel.

This story provides background for Paul's letter to the Ephesians, perhaps Paul's most beautiful depiction of the church, the body of all true believers from the time of Christ to the present day, and beyond. It is interesting that his most developed metaphor in Ephesians is that of a temple. The people were proud of the temple of Artemis, and rightly so. But it does not compete with the one Paul describes, a temple made of disciples, spanning centuries, founded in Christ and the disciples, rising to dizzying heights. You and I are part of this temple. And unlike the temple of Artemis, of which only one pillar now remains, the temple of God's people will last eternally.

Finally one commentator explains that this chapter shows what happens when the gospel moves into a culture. To the extent the truth of the gospel is believed and practiced, culture is transformed. Darrell Bock writes, "This is the major unit in Acts showing how the transformation of a community affects the culture at large, making it so nervous that it reacts to stop the progress. What affects the commerce of idolatry in Ephesus is apparently not a program to stamp out magic but the change of lifestyle among believers." Has the gospel affected your life in radical ways, like it did those who worshiped Artemis? Is there anything taking up your resources that your love for Christ should change?

Read 20:1–12

Observe

Why does Paul decide to go back through Macedonia, where he had just been?

On what day of the week do the believers meet, and what things do they do?

Why does Paul preach for such a long time in Troas? What tragic event does this lead to?

Interpret

It says twice at the beginning of this chapter that Paul shared encouragement. Read verses 1–3 again. From what we have read in Acts, why do you think the disciples and new believers would have needed encouragement?

Verse 9 says the boy was "picked up dead," but in verse 10 Paul says "He's alive!" What do you think is going on here? Did Eutychus die or not?

Apply

Have you ever wondered why most churches meet on Sunday, when it was the last, not first, day of the week God set aside as a day of rest? In Acts 20:7 Paul speaks on the first day of the week at a special meeting. This is the first mention of such a gathering on a Sunday, and it is probable that the first Christians chose this day because Jesus resurrected and often appeared after the resurrection on the first day of the week.

This scene also records the first time someone falls asleep during a sermon! As Paul preaches into the night, Eutychus (whose name means "lucky one") falls out of a third story window. Eutychus was probably between 8 to 14 years of age. Although Paul seems to say that the young man is still alive after his fall (v. 10), he more likely means something like, "There is life for him yet." Verse 9, after all, says he was "picked up dead." What this means is that Paul raised this young man from the dead. This recalls deeds by Jesus raising the widow's son (Luke 7:11–15), Jairus's daughter Luke 8:49–56) and Lazarus (John 11:38–44). This is Paul's last miracle in Acts. The people see that the gospel does not just offer life in the age to come, but power over death in this life also.

We've seen ancient roots of our Sunday church gatherings and a display of God's power in the middle of the night, in the city of Troas, just before Paul leaves this city for good. *How does this passage speak to you today?*

Read 20:13–38

Observe

Paul's final words to the Ephesian elders is one of the longest speeches in Acts (vv. 18–35). Below briefly provide what you believe are his main thoughts to the elders:

Interpret

Looking back at these verses, how does Paul feel about the church of God that he is leaving under the care of the elders? What details from his speech tell you this?

What fear does Paul have about the future of the church of Ephesus (vv. 29–31)?

Apply

In this tearful departure, Paul is leaving the people he has worked for tirelessly. He has suffered persecution and hardship, and as he says, "not hesitated to preach anything that would be helpful [. . .] declared to both Jews and Greeks that they must turn to God in repentance and have faith in our Lord Jesus" (vv. 20–21). Paul's final words are stirring, especially because Paul did not just teach with words, but with his life. When we know someone who is loving, gracious, wise, self-sacrificial, greatly interested in our well-being, our hearts are drawn to those people, and we are heartbroken if they somehow leave our lives. This is how The Ephesian elders felt about Paul, as we can tell by their response at the end.

But that is not all that is here. Paul knows that people will begin to distort the truth of what he has taught them, some even from their own congregation (v. 30). Why does Paul care so much about this "flock" that had been under his care? Because they were "bought with his own blood" (v. 28). This is the only direct reference to Jesus's sacrifical work in Acts. It tells us that Paul sees the death of Christ as a purchase of those who would believe. And if the people are precious enough to God to purchase with his own blood, they are worthy of Paul's concern about the effect of future "savage wolves" (v. 29). Paul says that they will "distort the truth" in order to make disciples (v. 30). The word used here means "to twist" something, and its result stands in contrast to something that is straight and true.

Do you see fellow believers as Paul does, and have similar love for them as people Christ died to save? How can you make sure you stay true to believing the gospel Paul delivered?

Read 21:1–14

Observe

What city are Paul and his companions in at the beginning of this passage, and what city are they in at the end?

This passage contains two scenes with similar events. What two scenes are these, and what similarities do you notice about these two sections?

What warning does Paul receive in each section, and from whom?

Interpret

What does it seem that Paul's primary goal is, according to this passage?

Read Luke 9:51–53. How does it relate to the passage for today?

Apply

Verses 1–3 record what is probably a 6–10 day journey at sea. At this phase in his journeys Paul continues to move closer to Jerusalem at each stage. In Tyre Paul encounters the followers of Jesus, the disciples who live in that region. By this time Phoenicia (the coastal region that contained Tyre) already had a Christian presence for about 20 years. These disciples plead with Paul not to go to Jerusalem. Similarly, in Caesarea a prophet named Agabus gives an even sterner warning, and a memorable, visual one. But Paul is determined to go to Jerusalem. Paul says he is willing to die for the Lord in Jerusalem. There is no dissuading Paul on this point.

Have you ever felt God calling you to do something that others question, perhaps even trying to dissuade you from something you believe the Lord wants you to do? This passage shows that sometimes good, godly people (even a godly prophet, in this passage!) can stand as obstacles to your acting in faith and according to your own conscience. The people love Paul, and they fear for his safety. This is understandable. But Paul knew his physical safety was not his highest priority. Are there any things God has placed on your heart to do that well-meaning people have been keeping you from doing?

Read 21:15-40

Observe (verses 27-40)

What do the people think Paul had done that makes them so angry? Was he guilty of this?

Who comes to rescue Paul?

What surprises the Roman soldiers about Paul?

What does Paul want to do

Interpret

Why do you think the crowd is so angry about what they think Paul has done? How would you describe Paul's attitude in these verses?

Apply

Paul now makes his defense before the hostile crowd. The fact that he is speaking in Aramaic tells us it's not meant for the Romans, but for the Jews. The word "defense" in verse 1 is the Greek word *apologia*, from which we get the word "apologetics." So Paul is defending his actions in bringing the gospel to the Gentiles. It may be strange for us to think that the Jewish people of Paul's day would be upset that Christianity is being taught to non-Jews, since we think of Christianity mainly as a non-Jewish faith. But in Paul's day there was no sense that Christinaity was for non-Jews. All the first Christians were Jews. It was not seen as another religion at all, but as the true Jewish faith (by people like post-conversion Paul and the other believers) or as a perversion of the Jewish faith (by this crowd).

Why does Paul tell the people he used to persecute Christians? He wants them to see that he believed as they did, but he changed. No one could accuse Paul of being ignorant or apathetic about his beliefs. He was educated under the highly respected Gamaliel and was "zealous" for God (v. 3). In fact he was probably even more zealous, since he describes himself as arresting men and women and throwing them into prison. But he wants the people to know that God did something in his life that stopped him in his tracks and led to a radical change (vv. 6–16). This defining moment in Paul's life explains everything he has done since.

We now see that Paul was not only unafraid of the danger he would face in Jerusalem, but actually saw it as an opportunity. Instead of running in fear, he has turned a dangerous situation into an opportunity to tell a huge crowd the story of what God has done in his life. This is essentially what sharing the gospel is: telling others what God has done in your life. You don't need to know everything about the Bible or the answers to every question. Even Paul did not know it all. But he did know how God had changed his life. Do you know how God has changed your life?

Read 22:17–29

Observe

Paul continues to tell the angry crowd the story of his conversion. What does he say the Lord says to him when he (Paul) shares his concern that the believers will remember him as the one who had Stephen stoned?

What does Paul say that puts the Jews over the edge with anger? Why does it have this effect?

What does the centurion decide to do to Paul because of the effect Paul has had on them? How does Paul respond to the centurion?

Interpret

What positive effect could it have on the angry Jewish people to know that Paul had led the stoning of Stephen, and that this fact made him doubtful of being able to talk to the believers?

Why do you think the author of Acts (Luke) decides to include the short exchange about Romans citizenship (vv. 27–29)?

Apply

Here Paul continues his defense of his ministry to the Gentiles. Remember, all of this started because of a lie about Paul, that he had taken Gentiles into the temple area. However, he uses this as an opportunity to explain why he has brought the message of Christ to the Gentiles. To the Jews, it seems as though he is inviting Gentiles to practice Judaism, and also promoting Jesus's claims to be the promised Messiah.

Paul reiterates the story of his conversion. Was Paul looking for attention when he turned to Christ? Did he have some need to stand out from the crowd, be a contrarian, or ruffle feathers? No. He wants the Jews to know that not only was he a good practicing Pharisee, but he was the most ambitious and driven Pharisee of them all, to the point that he organized and approved of the stoning of Stephen (Acts 8). He is saying to the Jews, "If you think you are committed to keeping Judaism pure, just listen to my story." The implication is that Paul had been stopped in his tracks (literally) by Christ, and he is inviting the Jewish people to become followers of Christ as well.

Paul's past was not good. He had done some terrible things, things to be ashamed of. But God does not just tell Paul "get over it." God will use Paul's past in his unique plan for him (v. 21). He will send Paul to the Gentiles. Your past is not perfect either. What are some ways your past could lead to unique opportunities for you to share the gospel? What kinds of people might listen to you in particular because of the things you have done or experienced?

Read 22:30–23:22

Observe

What does Paul say that angers the high priest?

Recall: What is the difference between the Pharisees and the Sadducees regarding the resurrection of the dead?

What does the Lord say to Paul about his plan for the future?

Interpret

Why do you think what Paul said to the high priest angered him so much?

What are some of the ways God's plan is at work in this tumultuous passage?

Apply

In the very middle of this passage is an incredible scene. In verse 11 it says that the Lord stood near Paul and told him that he would testify next in Rome. What makes this amazing is that it does not say an angel said this, but the Lord himself. In verse 9 the Pharisees (who believed in a resurrection of the dead) excuse Paul by saying, "What if a spirit or an angel has spoken to him?" That indeed would be incredible, but the truth is much more amazing: the Lord himself has been speaking to Paul, telling him what his plan is and what to do next. If just invoking the name of God was worthy of a punch in the face (v. 2), Paul's revealing that God had spoken to him would have infuriated the Sanhedrin. He would have been killed for sure. God's speaking directly to Paul seems to put him on the same level as Moses, who "knew the Lord face to face."

So what is it that God reveals? That Paul is to be taken to Rome next, in order to testify there just as he has in Jerusalem. Although Paul had usually stayed in cities for months or even years, his time in Jerusalem has been short. In fact there is only one account of Paul speaking to the people at all (22:1–21). Paul has become an explosive and polarizing figure, because of his message. At the end of the chapter we learn that the Jews (40 of them!) had secretly planned to murder Paul. Paul's nephew learns of this and warns Paul, who warns the commander, and in this way Paul is to be taken to safety in Rome. This means that the conspiracy against Paul worked according to God's plan, to fulfill exactly what he wanted—making sure Paul was taken to Rome. God will probably not appear to you like he did to Paul, what we can learn from this. Are there things in your life that seem to be going very wrong–maybe even unjust things–that you should recognize as part of God's plan in your life?

Read 23:23–24:9

Observe

What action does the commander take in order to protect Paul?

In his letter to Governor Felix, what does the commander say was the reason he brought Paul before the Sanhedrin?

What order does the commander say he has given to Paul's accusers?

When the high priest arrives before Felix to give his charges against Paul, what are those charges?

Interpret

What are some of the ways Paul's experiences in these scenes echo those of Jesus?

What do you think of the charges the high priest presents to Felix? Are they valid? How do you think Paul will defend himself?

Apply

It may be difficult to get a sense of how dramatic the events of these chapters are. Let's review. The plot against Paul involved 40 men (40 against 1!). Fortunately Paul's nephew hears of it, and the Roman commander takes action to protect Paul, in the form of 470 men! They are to accompany Paul to Caesarea, where he is to stand trial before Governor Felix. By this time Paul must have been known throughout the Roman world. It makes sense to ask why are this trouble is taking place over someone like Paul. It is hard to imagine him a threat. We know from other sources that he was probably short, bald, and had a vision problem. Why is Paul so feared?

This is exactly the question the commander wants to know, and why he commands that the high priest himself travel to Caesarea to answer for his actions against Paul. The high priest starts by praising the governor's ability to keep peace and thanking him for this. Then the high priest explains his case against Paul. He charges that (among other things) Paul has stirred up riots all over the world. But is this the problem the high priest really has against Paul? One has to ask, what caused the riots? The answer is that the Jewish people in these places did not agree with Paul's ministry to the Gentiles. They did not believe that the Judaism Paul was preaching (which of course featured Jesus as the promised messiah) should be open to just anyone. We must admire Paul's boldness in doing God's will. It is hard to find someone with more commitment to the Lord in all the Bible, except for Jesus. It is also a challenge to see how Paul's love for Christ comes out in his boldness to teach the truth and his unwavering willingness to face danger to show love to the people by teaching them the gospel.

Read 24:10–27

Observe

In making his defense before Governor Felix, what accusations against him does Paul deny? What accusations does he own up to?

At the end of his speech, Paul gives a possible explanation as to why the Sanhedrin thinks him guilty of a crime. What is that "crime?"

What is Paul's situation at the end of this chapter, and for how long?

Interpret

The phrase "the Way" is mentioned in this passage, in verse 14 and verse 22. What do you think is meant by this phrase?

Why do you think it says that Felix was "afraid" in verse 25?

Apply

This section ends on a surprising note. Did you notice that Paul was left in prison for two years? On one hand it may have seemed like a waste of his time for Paul. We think of him as proactive, constantly on the move, always thinking ahead. On the other hand, Paul says in Philippians 4:11, "I have learned to be content whatever the circumstances," and he knew he was going to face arrest before he came to Jerusalem. We can imagine Paul perfectly at peace, engaged in worship, looking for opportunity to share the gospel with anyone God brought his way.

Finally, another theme emerges, if you read carefully. Notice that Felix ends the conversation with Paul at a key moment. Verse 25 says that when Paul starts to talk about righteousness, self-control, and jugement, Felix wants Paul to stop, and dismisses him (though he does visit frequently after this). Is this a good moment for Felix? Does it show he has a conscience? Not necessarily, since it says that he was afraid and wanted to hear no more. If Felix had felt guilty perhaps he would have changed his ways. But his fear does not seem to lead to repentance. Instead he continues to visit Paul not to learn from him, but hoping to receive a bribe. But this is not the first time in the passage the theme of conscience is raised. In verse 16 Paul says that he always strives "to keep my conscience clear before God and man." We are meant to see a contrast between Paul and Felix. Since, as Paul says, there will be a resurrection of both the righteous and the wicked, may we strive to keep a clear conscience as well."

Read 25:1–12

Observe

When Festus, the new governor travels to Jerusalem, what do the Jewish leaders ask him to do, and why?

Festus refuses this request. What does he suggest they do instead?

Why does Paul say he is unwilling to go to Jerusalem to face the charges of the Jewish leaders?

Interpret

Why do you think the Jewish leaders are so determined to kill Paul?

Why do you think Paul demands to stand trial before Caesar (v. 11)?

Apply

The author Luke continues to describe the ordeal Paul is facing in a way that reminds us of the trial and crucifixion of Christ. Just like Jesus went from the high priest to Pilate to Herod, Paul has gone from Felix to Festus, and next, to Caesar. There are other similarities too. Jesus and Paul both stood before Roman authorities because they were accused of breaking religious laws. The Romans were not in charge of enforcing Jewish law; this would be like telling a police officer that your friend was using vulgar language. He would probably say, "I'm sorry to hear that, but it's not illegally, and quite frankly, not my business." But here we see a third similarity. Both Pilate and Festus want to please the Jews. Of course, the Romans were occupying Israel, and did not really need the Jews to like them. But it helped to keep the Jewish leaders happy, if possible. Similarly, how often do we compromise doing the right thing in order to find favor with the people around us? Pilate and Festus both had the chance to stand for what is right, but neither of them did.

Finally, notice Paul's single-minded determination in this passage. The Jewish leaders want him to come back to Jerusalem in order to ambush him. Paul may suspect this plot–he already knows they want to kill him. But there is another reason he requests to stand trial before Caesar: he wants to tell him about Jesus. We already know Paul is not afraid to die; in fact he says that again here (v. 11). But while the Jewish leaders are chasing Paul, Paul is chasing God's will for his life. There will be people in your life who want to discourage you, even stop you from doing what you believe the Lord wants you to do. Some of these people may even have good intentions, such as friends or family members. Paul sets a good example. He does not get caught up in disputing the Jewish leaders or defending himself. Instead he makes a decision that will allow him to keep on track. He is heading to Rome.

Read 25:13–27

Observe

Festus is telling the story of Paul to King Agrippa. For what reason does Festus not condemn Paul to death?

What does Festus say about Jesus?

Instead of going back to Jerusalem to face his accusers, what does Paul elect to do?

Interpret

Why do you think King Agrippa says he would like to hear from Paul himself, after hearing the story about Paul's imprisonment and appeal to Caesar (v. 22)?

Why do you think Luke records several times that Paul had not broken Roman law?

Apply

We already know that Paul was not arrested for breaking any Roman laws. In fact he did not even break Jewish laws, he was only accused of doing so. And yet Luke, the author, continues to nail this point down as he records the words of Festus to King Agrippa. In verse 18 he says "they did not charge him with any of the crimes I had expected," in verse 25 he says "he had done nothing deserving of death," and in verse 27, "I think it unreasonable to send on a prisoner without specifying the charges against him." To King Agrippa, Paul is an innocent man who has gotten caught up in a dangerous religious dispute. According to Roman law he could be set free immediately, but instead he appeals to Caesar. One would stand before Caesar on capital charges (those deserving of death), and this is why Festus feels the need to explain that he is sending Paul because of Paul's request, and not because Paul deserves it. Festus must think it crazy that Paul has made this decision, but to Paul it makes all the sense in the world.

In Matthew 10, Jesus sends out the disciples to share the good news. He warns them about some of the things they will experience. Take a moment to read Matthew 10:16-20 and consider: we often try to avoid the pain and discomfort described here, but perhaps we should embrace it, as part of our decision to be followers of Christ.

Read 26:1–23

Observe

Starting in verse 4, list the main points of Paul's defense before King Agrippa:

Interpret

Paul says that he too was convinced he should do all he could to appose Jesus (v. 9). According to this passage, what changes this for Paul?

According to Paul, how is true faith demonstrated? What do you think he means by this?

What role does Scripture play in Paul's defense?

Apply

By now we are familiar with Paul's defense. He used to persecute the Christians, but now he has gone from being the most zealous Pharisee to the most zealous Christian. As a pharisee, violence, intimidation, and murder were part of his program, but these are not part of his life as a zealous Christian, even though he is just as committed to his cause. Paul's defense of that most unpopular emphasis of his ministry–reaching the Gentiles–is that Jesus himself appeared to Paul and gave him his mission.

Chances are Jesus has not appeared to you in the way he did to Paul, giving you a special mission that you could not deny, that compels you as it did the Apostle Paul. But guess what–you and I have something even more compelling, even more sure, even more reliable that what Paul had. In 2 Peter 1:19, Peter says we have "the prophetic word made more sure." What does he mean by this? Peter had seen Jesus, of course. But in one special instance, Peter had seen Jesus as he really was, even as Paul had seen him. Peter saw Jesus's glory unveiled on the mountain (Mt. 17:1-8). And yet, Peter says that God's word is "more sure," "more reliable."

You may not have people actually seeking your arrest, but chances are you do experience those who would prefer you to follow their ways instead of God's, just like the pharisees did Paul. Like Paul, may you hold on to God's revealed will for your life, whether it is reaching out to a person others are being mean to, or avoiding substances that those around you have normalized, or whatever poses a contrast between God's sure word to you in scripture and the opinions of those around you.

Read 26:24–27:20

Observe

What is Paul's wish for King Agrippa and for all those listening? Does King Agrippa believe Paul deserves to be imprisoned?

Beginning in 27:1, where is Paul being taken, and why?

What warning of Paul does the centurion not follow?

Interpret

What do you think Festus means when he says, "Do you think in such a short time you can persuade me to be a Christian?" (v. 28). Why does he say this?

Verses 3–8 contain a lot of information about where Paul's ship was sailing and about different places in the Mediterranean. Notice how the passage ends (v. 20). What do you think is the purpose of sharing this information?

Apply

Many well-known stories involve adventures at sea and long descriptions using nautical terms, similar to what we see in chapter 27. To name a few these include *Moby Dick, Treasure Island, Gulliver's Travels,* and perhaps the very first adventure at sea, *The Odyssey,* which takes place on the Mediterranean as well. What makes these adventures exciting is the mission that is jeopardized by catastrophe–whether hunting a white whale, looking for buried treasure, or just trying to get home to wife and son.

What is the mission here? Paul wants to appear before the emperor of the civilized world, Caesar himself, in order to share the gospel. This is why he went to Jerusalem instead of going the other direction, why he appealed to Rome instead of going free. And now the danger has increased–not only do Jews want to kill him, but the sea and wind themselves are putting him and his crew at risk. Paul says conditions are bad because it is after the Day of Atonement. Beginning in the month of October, conditions were very bad on the Mediterranean. Most people would think it foolish even to attempt a journey to Rome during this time. Remember, there was no doppler radar, no reliable forecast about conditions at sea. They were taking a great risk. Our passage ends with a cliffhanger: they have gotten rid of most of their cargo (including tackle, which they threw over "with their own hands!") and are no longer navigating. Instead, they are drifting aimlessly, hoping somehow to survive. It must have seemed like God was no longer in control of this journey. Have you ever felt like nobody is in control at steering wheel of your life? Perhaps drifting, enduring bad things that keep coming, maybe wondering if God even exists? Paul had to wait and trust God, as he is at the end of this section, and often, we will need to do the same.

Read 27:21–44

Observe

What message does Paul receive from the angel that he delivers to the men on board?

How many people are on board the ship?

Why does Paul say it is important that all the men stay with the ship?

Interpret

How would you describe the role Paul is playing on board the ship? Has it changed since the journey to Rome began?

In what ways is this story similar to the book of Jonah? How does it differ?

Apply

The description of this leg of Paul's journey to Rome may or may not strike you with terror, but it should. Having been caught in hurricane-like conditions south of Italy, the crew has given up any attempt to steer the ship. They have also been forced to throw many valuable things overboard, including the fishing tackle that would provide them with more food. But it gets even worse. Several of the crew members attempt to escape by secretly lowering a life boat. Paul catches them in the act and tells the centurion that their lives hang in the balance: he has had a vision that they will be saved and he will reach Caesar, but no one must desert this ship.

This suggests an interesting interplay between God's will and our actions. Paul has already been promised that no one would be lost (v. 22), and yet he says that unless everyone stays aboard the ship they will die (v. 31). Here we see at work something like what he writes in Philippian 2:12–13. He says to "work out your salvation," but that "it is God who works in you." On the one hand God does it all, but on the other hand we must work as well. When Paul was told of God's will for this ship, he did not sit back and let that plan happen. Instead, he worked to accomplish God's plan. That is a different approach than the one we might naturally take. We may tend to sit back and let God's will happen (fatalism) or, thinking it is all up to us, scrutinize every tiny decision, believing our future depends only on our own actions (paralysis). The truth is that there is room for God's will and our own actions, as we see from Paul here.

Finally, notice that Paul's ship is in danger because he is obeying God, whereas Jonah endangered his crew by disobeying. The men sailing for Tarsus know God is angry, but they are not sure who to blame. Jonah finally tells them that it is him. Paul, on the other hand, does the opposite. Because of Paul's obedience the whole crew is promised safety to Rome. Is your relationship with God bringing others blessing, like Paul, or cursing, like Jonah?

Read 28:1–16

Observe

What do the men of Malta assume at first about Paul when a poisonous snake bits his hand? What makes them change their minds?

In what ways does Paul minister to the people of Malta while he is there? How long does he stay?

When they finally arrive in Rome, who has come to greet Paul?

Interpret

We already know that Paul has set his mind on reaching Rome, just as Jesus "set his face toward Jerusalem" (Luke 9:52). With that in mind, why do you think Paul spent so much time on the island of Malta?

One commentator has written that "the most important theme of the passage is that God can be taken at his word" (Darrell Bock). How do we see this truth in today's passage?

Apply

If you visit the island of Malta today, located 58 miles south of Italy and 180 miles northeast of Africa, you will find the Bay of St. Paul. This bay, of course, pays homage to the 2,000-year-old story you just read, the very spot where Paul's ship landed and the events of Paul's snakebite and ministry on Malta unfolded. Although there are no poisonous snakes on the island today, they were obviously there in Paul's day. At first it must have seemed ironic to the people—here a prisoner of Rome escapes shipwreck only to be killed on a seemingly safe island. He must be guilty for sure! But when he shakes off the poisonous serpent and the people see that the bite had no effect on Paul (Mark 16:18), the people assume he is a god. From other passages we know that Paul would not like to be thought of as either a god or a criminal, and he was neither. In order for him to have a ministry of the gospel to the people, they needed to see that he had not broken Roman law and that he was merely a man saved by God's grace.

It is surprising that Paul spends three months on Malta, considering that the entire journey takes four months. We don't have a letter to Malta like we do for Ephesus, Rome, or Corinth, but people believed Paul's message there. In the ancient world it was typical for the visitor to be treated with hospitality (*xenia*), as you may have read in Homer's *Odyssey*. But here it is Paul who is the tremendous blessing. He doesn't start by sharing the gospel, but by befriending the people and meeting needs. *What are some of the ways you can bring blessing to the people in your community?*

Finally, we should note how amazing it is that Paul's ship found this tiny island. Malta is only eight miles wide, and the ship was sailing without being steered, drifting aimlessly in the storm. And yet it found Malta, like finding a needle in a haystack. God can be taken at his word. The ship ran aground, no lives were lost, and Paul reached Rome. *What do you need to trust God about today?* He can be trusted, 100%.

Read 28:17–31

Observe

Who does Paul first meet with?

Paul explains the circumstances under which he has arrived in Rome. Are the Jews in Rome opposed to him, as those in Judea were? Why or why not?

What does Paul say that causes the Jewish people to depart?

Interpret

How is Paul's activity here in Rome similar to what he has done in the other cities he has visited?

Why do you think the Jewish people begin to leave after Paul quotes from Isaiah?

The book ends with Paul still under house arrest in Rome. What is he doing with his time there? Finally, why do you think the book ends with Paul still in a Roman prison?

Apply

Paul's approach to Rome is like that in other cities, where he goes first to the synagogues and then opens his message to Gentiles. He still thinks of the Jews as his brothers and sisters in the faith. On the other hand, he is clear that they are missing the fulfillment of the Old Testament, and in this case, quoting from Isaiah, shows that their rejection was predicted. It is not surprising that some of them were offended and began to leave. Paul did not shy away from stating the truth, no matter how offensive it might have been to his listeners. *Are there things you believe that you should be more bold in saying? Are there ways you have quieted the truth in your heart so you don't upset others, stay popular and well-liked, etc.?*

As you can see from the final verses, Acts has an open ending. It does not record Paul standing before Emperor Nero, which he has been hoping to do for so many chapters. On the other hand, it records for us the seeds of Paul's ministry in Rome, which would become the seat of Christianity in the West. Paul has arrived in the most important city in the ancient world, and he makes the best possible use of his time, renting a house, where he "preached the kingdom of God and taught about the Lord Jesus Christ" (v. 31).

As we close our study we end with these final insights from Darrell Bock about the book of Acts: "All of this is the work of an active God. God has been directing events throughout the book. God set forth the call for the mission. God gave the Spirit. God directed the church to the Gentiles. God called out Paul with Barnabas and then sent Paul to Jerusalem and Rom. God protected Paul as he brought the word there as God's faithful witness. God can be trusted, and his calling is to be followed. Paul shows us that the combination of divine aid and humans' faithfulness to God's calling is powerful." May you combine faithfulness to God with his divine aid, and continue the work of the gospel that started in Acts!